First Steps in Inclusion

Stephanie Lorenz

David Fulton Publishers
London

This book is dedicated to all the parents who have been prepared to take on the educational establishment in their fight for inclusive education.

David Fulton Publishers Ltd
Ormond House, 26–27 Boswell Street, London WC1N 3JZ

www.fultonpublishers.co.uk

First published in Great Britain by David Fulton Publishers 2002

British Library Cataloguing in Publication Data
A catalogue record for this book is available from the British Library.

ISBN 1–85346–763–4

Typeset by Elite Typesetting Techniques, Eastleigh, Hampshire
Printed and bound in Great Britain by Bell and Bain Ltd, Glasgow

Contents

Acknowledgements

For me, this book marks a significant milepost on the journey towards a truly inclusive educational system, with amendments to Section 316 of the 1996 Education Act strengthening parents' rights to a mainstream place and the SEN & Disability Act outlawing discriminatory practice in schools. Yet there is still a very long way to go before the needs of all children can be successfully met in the mainstream.

In compiling this book, I have drawn on the experiences of the many parents, teachers and learning supporters who I have been lucky enough to work with over the last seven years. Their commitment and vision have kept me going. I have also gained inspiration from the work of Linda Shaw at CSIE, Micheline Mason and her colleagues in the Alliance for Inclusive Education, Jack Pierpoint and Marsha Forrest from Canada, Colin Newton and Derek Wilson from Inclusive Solutions and all my colleagues in the Down's Syndrome Educational Consortium.

Particular thanks are due to Michael Giangreco and Mary Beth Doyle, whose recent seminar gave me much cause for thought and to Anne Hutchinson from Hedgewood School, who first introduced me to the idea of Curriculum Mapping. I am grateful to all three for allowing me to include aspects of their work.

At the draft stage, valuable feedback was obtained from Sally Capper and Eric Nicholas from the Down's Syndrome Association and from Trish Dawson, Head of Pupil Services in Bury. The chapter for parents was scrutinised by Janice Pickering, Jan Butler and Cathy Davies, all parents of children with Special Educational Needs who have personal experience of the battle for effective inclusion. The early years section was read by Claire Barker, head teacher of a nursery school in Bury, and Amy Lorenz, reception class teacher from Lincoln, both of whom made helpful comments.

Assistance on the management chapters was received from Nick Briscoe, a primary head from Cheshire, and Ros Davies, a former secondary deputy from Leicester. As an experienced SENCO she was also immensely helpful on the SENCO chapter, as was Marie Webb from Oldham. Finally, thanks are due to the numerous LSAs who have helped develop the chapter for learning supporters, particularly Gill Forshaw, secondary LSA from Wigan, and Joy Potter, primary LSA from Cheshire.

As always the staff at David Fulton have been courteous and helpful, while keeping me on schedule, despite unforeseen delays in the passage of the new legislation, and my husband Roger has encouraged and cajoled me to complete what has proved to be a surprisingly difficult book to write.

My thanks go to them all.

Chapter 1

Introduction

What do we mean by inclusion?

'Inclusion' is undoubtedly the buzz word of the decade. Everywhere you turn there are policies and mission statements about services and organisations becoming ever more inclusive. With each group using the term in its own way, it is not surprising that people are becoming confused. Even within the educational world, interpretations of what exactly is and isn't inclusive education vary widely and many have very little to do with equality of opportunity or universal access to mainstream education. For the purposes of this book, the term 'inclusion' will be used for the successful mainstreaming of pupils with special educational needs (SEN) who would traditionally have been placed in special schools. Our emphasis will be on celebrating diversity and responding positively to the challenges that are presented.

Mercia prides itself on being an inclusive local education authority (LEA). The majority of pupils with statements are supported in their local mainstream school. At the same time, it has a well funded and highly regarded network of special schools for pupils with severe learning difficulties. Pupils are assessed preschool, and on the basis of their ability are offered either a mainstream or a special school place. Tom's parents accept that he has severe learning difficulties, nevertheless they are convinced that he should attend a mainstream school. After approaching seven local schools who all said 'no', they found a welcoming school. Despite this, the LEA held their position and insisted that special school was the only appropriate placement.

Q. Is this a truly inclusive LEA?

A. No it isn't. In any inclusive system, all children are valued equally and are welcomed into the mainstream. Their school place is theirs of right and is not conditional on their level of need.

Hampton LEA state in their mission statement their commitment to inclusive education. While a high proportion of pupils with statements continue to be placed in segregated settings, the LEA has devolved Standards Fund money to their special schools to enable as many children as possible to attend a mainstream school on a part-time basis, thus getting 'the best of both worlds'. Each child on the programme attends a mainstream school for a maximum of one half day per week.

Q. Is this inclusion?

A. No it isn't. Children who are included should be on the roll of a mainstream school and attend on a full-time basis.

Niamh is very small for her age and is significantly delayed in her development. At four she was not yet toilet trained, so her school decided to keep her down in the nursery. At six she was only speaking in single words and was working towards Level 1 of the National Curriculum, so she was kept down again. At eight she is still in a class of five-and six-year-olds. At her last review, the school was pleased to report that she now fitted in so well, both academically and socially, you hardly knew she was there.

Q. Is this inclusion?

A. No it isn't. If children are to gain a sense of their own identity and benefit from age-appropriate models of learning and behaviour, they must mix regularly with typical peers of their own age. Keeping children down may seem to solve an immediate problem, but it is likely to cause greater difficulties in the long term.

Tariq is a bright little boy with Down's Syndrome. In his LEA, children like Tariq who are assessed as having 'moderate learning difficulties' are placed in a resourced mainstream school. Each morning Tariq registers in the special unit and then, after sitting with the other unit children during assembly, spends the rest of each morning withdrawn for literacy and numeracy. Since his special taxi rarely arrives at school before 9 a.m. there is no time for him to play with his mainstream friends before school. While he joins with typically developing peers for music, art and PE, he is not with them every day because some days there is no one available to support him in class, so he goes back to the unit.

Q. Is Tariq being included?

A. No he isn't. As full and equal members of the school community included pupils should be given the opportunity to learn and play alongside their mainstream peers for most of the school day.

Ricardo is profoundly deaf and relies on British Sign Language as his primary form of communication. He has settled well into Year 7 of his local high school with in-class support from a signing interpreter. At the school's open evening for prospective new pupils, Year 7 pupils were invited to attend and to befriend a visiting student, showing them round the school. Because of possible communication problems, the school decided it would be unfair on

Ricardo to ask him to do this. No one consulted him or his parents – he just didn't get an invitation.

Q. Is this inclusion?

A. No it isn't. As a member of the school community, an included student should have the opportunity to participate fully in the non-curricular life of the school as well as in the academic curriculum. The issue isn't whether he should participate, but what support he needs to enable him do so.

Tamara is partially sighted and attends her local secondary school where she is doing well academically. However, she is finding it difficult to get around the large campus and to cope on crowded staircases. Her parents have asked for additional mobility training and for her to be let out of lessons early. These requests have been refused as the school say that inclusion means being treated the same as everyone else.

Q. Are they right?

A. No they aren't. While included children should have full access to the curriculum and the life of the school, inclusion does not mean that their individual needs are ignored or special help refused.

Sally has cerebral palsy. To make her local secondary school fully accessible would have involved time and effort as well as some additional expenditure, which the school was reluctant to commit, so she was offered a place in a newly adapted school 15 miles from her home. Each morning she is collected by taxi and taken to school. Her friends all live around the school so she never sees them in her local shops or in the park at weekends. When it was her birthday, she invited all the girls in her tutor group to her party. Sadly, hardly anyone could come, as few of their parents have cars and local bus services are poor.

Q. Is Sally being fully included?

A. No she isn't. Effective educational inclusion should lead to community inclusion. Wherever possible, an inclusive school placement should allow young people to make relationships with others from the area where they live. Ideally they should go to their local school. Where this is not a realistic option, they should always be offered a school within reasonable travelling distance of home.

So what *is* truly inclusive education? (See Figure 1.1)

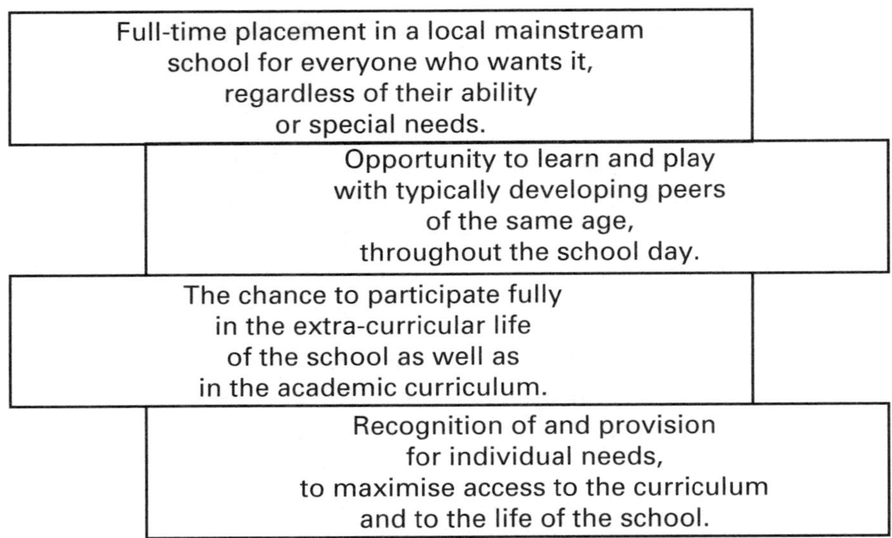

Figure 1.1 What is inclusive education?

What the law and the government say

Until January 2002 LEAs and schools were working to the requirements of the Education Act 1996, while having regard to the *Code of Practice on the Identification and Assessment of Special Educational Needs* (Department for Education and Employment (DfEE) 1994). Within the law as it stood, the LEA had a qualified duty to 'secure that the child is educated in a school that is not a special school unless that is incompatible with the wishes of his parents'. They could only deny a parental preference if they believed the school was unable to meet the child's needs, or would be incompatible with the education of other children or the efficient use of resources.

Before naming a school, the law also stated that the LEA must consult the governors. Guidance from the Code of Practice noted that: 'the LEA should give due consideration to the views expressed by those consulted, but the final decision as to whether to name the school falls to the LEA'. Despite this, LEAs rarely considered it appropriate to override the governors and direct reluctant mainstream schools to admit pupils with a statement of SEN.

The Code of Practice undoubtedly provided a framework within which inclusion could be promoted. But it soon became clear that it could do little on its own to change entrenched positions. The newly elected Labour Government of 1997, therefore, with its professed commitment to increase inclusion, set about reviewing practice. In its consultation document *Excellence for All Children: Meeting Special Educational Needs* (DfEE 1997) it states:

> We want to see more pupils with SEN included in mainstream primary and secondary schools. By inclusion we mean not only that pupils with SEN should wherever possible receive their education in a mainstream school, but also that they should join fully with their peers in the curriculum and life of the school.

> For example, we believe that . . . children with SEN should generally take part in mainstream lessons rather than being isolated in separate units.

Regrettably, this document said nothing about the need for children to attend a neighbourhood school, which would allow them to make friends in their local community. Nevertheless, it went a lot further than previous government publications in encouraging more inclusive practices. It went on to say that for children with complex needs, the wide variation in opportunities to attend a mainstream school found across the country was unacceptable. In extolling LEAs to adopt more inclusive practices, it was encouraging to see the department stressing that 'It is not good enough simply to say that local mainstream schools have not previously included a child with these needs' as an excuse for failing to include a particular child. Instead the challenge was 'to identify the action that would be required and by whom, to make it happen'.

As well as looking at ways of fostering inclusion, the Programme of Action (DfEE 1998a) which followed the consultation document considered a range of other issues in SEN practice, including a revised Code of Practice which was first issued in draft form in July 2000. The aim was to have the new Code in place by September 2001. Although the time scales slipped somewhat, along with those for the publication of the SEN and Disability Act 2001, it eventually appeared in its final form in October 2001, with implementation in January 2002.

Both documents are likely to make a significant contribution to the inclusion debate. Within the new Code of Practice (DfES 2001), there is a clear statement that 'the Government believes that when parents want a mainstream place for their child the education service should do everything possible to try to provide it'. They go on to say that 'All schools should admit pupils with already identified special educational needs ... Admissions authorities for mainstream schools may not refuse to admit a child because they feel unable to cater for their special educational needs'.

This is a powerful statement, although in itself it has no real 'teeth'. However, the SEN and Disability Act now takes this somewhat further. In Part 1, the bill amends section 316 of the Education Act 1996 to state that a child with a statement of SEN: 'must be educated in a mainstream school unless this is incompatible with:

(a) the wishes of his parent; or
(b) the provision of efficient education for other children'.

Further, the Act states that an LEA can only rely on exception (b) 'if they show that there are no reasonable steps that they could take to prevent the incompatibility'. Even though this is somewhat less than the proponents of full inclusion had hoped for, it should be sufficient to allow more parents to succeed within the (SEN) Tribunal system in gaining an inclusive placement. Certainly it should no longer be possible for LEAs to say no to inclusion without making any effort to identify a suitable mainstream school, to work positively with school staff or to put in place the provision required to make the placement viable.

The effectiveness of any inclusive placement is, however, just as important as the placement itself. In its consultation document *From Exclusion to Inclusion*, published in 1999, the Disability Rights Task Force points out that 'inclusion is not only about attendance at a mainstream school. An inclusive curriculum is also essential'. Further, it stressed the need for legislation to overcome widespread discrimination in schools. These recommendations have now been enshrined in the SEN and Disability Act 2001.

This is a time both of challenge and opportunity. On the positive side:

- There are likely to be expectations and duties placed on LEAs and schools to make a greater effort to foster inclusion via clear policies, training initiatives and favourable resource allocations.
- Amendments to section 316 of the 1996 Education Act will strengthen the rights of parents to choose a mainstream school and the SEN and Disability Act 2001 should outlaw discriminatory practices within inclusive placements.

However:

- Recent statistics (Howson 2000) show that the number of children in special schools remains just below 10,000, around 1.3 per cent of the school population. As the author of the report comments, 'the full integration of pupils into mainstream schools still looks a great distance away'.
- Both the revised Code of Practice and the SEN and Disability Act 2001 have yet to be tested in the courts. Even with the amendment to section 316, LEAs will still be able, quite legally, to deny some individual pupils their right to a mainstream placement.

What research tells us

One of the difficulties experienced over the years by those advocating inclusive education is the continual pressure they face to prove that inclusion works. Yet at no stage has anyone ever been asked to prove the efficacy of special schooling. The assumption has always been that because it is special, with specially trained teachers and a high adult–child ratio, then it must obviously produce better results. Anecdotes abound but do little to clear the air. For each example of an included child who has thrived and benefited enormously from the experience, there is another epitomising mainstream failure, with the child being rescued by a benevolent special school.

Clearly experiments cannot be set up in which a population of children is placed randomly in special and mainstream schools to compare the long-term effects. Neither is it easy to match groups of children in different settings. Factors that influence placement decisions, e.g. social class, parental education or the ability level of the child, will also affect educational and social outcomes for pupils with special needs. Thus comparisons may be dangerous.

Nevertheless, there is now a small but growing body of research evidence that is beginning to point towards the benefits of inclusion over special schooling. The most significant is probably that produced by Professor Sue Buckley and her colleagues (Buckley *et al.* 2000), who have compared two populations of young people with Down's Syndrome in Hampshire. For historical reasons, almost all those children living in one area of the county, close to the Sarah Duffen Centre, have spent their whole school career to date in the mainstream. On the other hand, the contrast group, in another part of Hampshire with little experience of inclusion, have largely been placed in special schools for pupils with moderate learning difficulties (MLD) or severe learning difficulties (SLD).

Although the sample of 46 is relatively small, the results are of sufficient importance to detail here. First, they found that teenagers who had attended mainstream schools were significantly more advanced than their special school contemporaries in:

(a) expressive language (being on average 2 years 6 months ahead)
(b) reading (being around 3 years 4 months ahead)
(c) writing
(d) arithmetic (except money knowledge where there was no difference) and
(e) general knowledge.

No significant differences were found between the two groups with reference to daily living skills or social independence, although those in the mainstream appeared to be making fewer meaningful relationships with peers than their special school contemporaries. The authors of the study attribute this to the paucity of peers with learning difficulties in mainstream settings and conclude that the solution is to include a greater number of disabled pupils, thus giving those with disabilities a wider choice of friends.

Sadly, comparative research on other groups of pupils in the UK is hard to find. However, some small-scale studies do exist. Dew-Hughes and Blandford looked at the social development and independent learning skills of 12 children with severe learning difficulties in SLD or mainstream placements (Dew-Hughes and Blandford 1998; Dew-Hughes 1999). They found that the children in the mainstream were able to work cooperatively and autonomously for up to 300 per cent longer than their special school peers. While it is not clear how similar the two groups were in ability or in their profile of adaptive skills, it is the authors' view that the differences were due largely to teacher expectations, with teachers in the special schools giving their pupils less responsibility and having lower expectations for age-appropriate behaviours and social maturity.

In a similar vein, Beadman (1997) found in the Devon special schools she visited that there was less emphasis on teaching reading than in mainstream schools and less material for the teaching of reading. However, there is no need for complacency as there is no doubt that much poor practice also goes on in the name of inclusion. A recent study by the Royal National Institute for the Blind (RNIB) entitled *Shaping the Future* (2000) found that blind and partially sighted children attending mainstream schools are often given educational materials in a format they cannot read, rather than large print, audio tape or braille. Twenty-three per cent of their sample frequently failed to get accessible handouts or worksheets and 31 per cent received inaccessible test papers.

Despite the limited research evidence to support inclusion and real concerns about the inclusiveness of some existing provision, there is no doubt that a growing number of informed parents are seeking mainstream placements for their disabled children. Organisations such as the RNIB and the Down's Syndrome Association are increasingly involved in promoting good inclusive practice. Even organisations such as Scope and the National Autistic Society, who run their own special schools, recognise that for many young people, good quality inclusive education is the way forward.

So what do we know about the key factors in achieving an effective inclusive placement? The first and most significant element is a positive school ethos. The second is the commitment of the parents to inclusion and their willingness to work positively with the school. Finally, however good the partnership between the school and the family, effective inclusion will be difficult to achieve without the support of the LEA. Not only does the school need to be guaranteed an appropriate resource package to meet the needs of the child, but they need to feel that their LEA will offer them relevant training and advice when problems arise.

Successful inclusion is very rarely about the individual child's particular difficulties and little to do with their measured IQ. Examples abound of children with very severe learning or physical difficulties benefiting enormously from mainstream placement. Kenn Jupp (1992), the head teacher of a school for pupils with SLD, decided that the only fair way to select children for his pilot inclusion project was to draw names out of a hat. Similar conclusions were drawn from the Somerset Inclusion Project (Thomas *et al.* 1998) where pupils from a residential special school were moved on a full-time basis into the mainstream. It was found that while the level of resourcing required by individuals varied widely, together with the degree to which the curriculum needed to be differentiated, there was no justification to deny certain children the opportunity to experience an inclusive placement while offering it to others.

This is highlighted by the fact that the pattern of inclusion varies enormously from one LEA to another. Attitudes towards pupils with emotional and behavioural problems (EBD) are particularly indicative of an LEA's commitment to inclusion. In recent years there has been a significant growth in the development of new special schools and off-site units, catering for a growing population of pupils unwelcome in the mainstream. Yet in Merton (Barrow 1998), the LEA's only off-site centre was closed in 1997 and, as referrals dropped, its only primary special school for pupils with EBD closed in 1998. Instead, resources were focused on supporting the majority of difficult-to-manage pupils in the mainstream. It seems unlikely that pupils in this LEA are any less disruptive than those elsewhere, yet exclusion rates in Merton have fallen sharply as has the number of pupils in the secondary EBD school. Evaluation suggests that Merton's inclusion policy is working to the benefit of pupils and schools alike.

Why families want inclusion

Although there has been concern in certain professional circles for many years as to the effectiveness of special schools and the denial of human rights resulting from compulsory segregation (Beresford and Tuckwell 1978), it is undoubtedly parental pressure that has had the greatest impact on the development of inclusive practices. Groups of parents such as 'Parents for Inclusion', set up as long ago as 1984, have been fighting for the right of all disabled children to attend a local mainstream school if that is their parents' wish.

For many families, the issue is essentially one of human rights, whereby disabled young people 'should never be forced to lead separate lives away from their families and communities' (Beresford and Tuckwell 1978). It is also about rejecting the medical model of deficit and treatment. Micheline Mason (2000), a special school 'survivor', was told never to give up hope because one day doctors would find a cure for her affliction. Yet her belief as a disabled child was that she was already fully human and in no need of a cure. What she did need, however, was to be accepted as she was and to belong. The need for their children to be accepted and valued for themselves is a theme that runs through much of the writing produced by parents of disabled children (Murray and Penman 1996).

When I first had Kim he was my son.
A year later he was epileptic and developmentally delayed.
At 18 months he had special needs and he was a special child.
He had a mild to moderate learning difficulty.
He was mentally handicapped.
I was told not to think about his future.
I struggled with all this.

By the time he was four he had special educational needs.
He was a statemented child.
He was dyspraxic, epileptic, developmentally delayed and had
complex communication problems.

Two years later, aged six, he was severely epileptic (EP),
cerebral palsied (CP) and had complex learning difficulties.
At eight he had severe intractable epilepsy with
associated communication problems.
He was showing a marked developmental regression.
He had severe learning difficulties.

At nine he came out of segregated schooling and
he slowly became my son again.

Never again will he be anything else but Kim – a son, a
brother, a friend, a pupil, a teacher, a person.

As Rob Long (1999) points out, 'Most children are unhappy and miserable without friends; they experience feelings of loneliness, rejection and anger'. Ask the average child why they like going to school and the answer is almost certain to contain something about playing or being with friends. These friendship patterns then extend beyond the school day and provide the child with companions to play with after school or in the holidays. For children attending segregated special schools or units, these extended friendship networks rarely develop and the child happily established in a social framework at school has no one to play with once they return home.

The experience of parents whose children are included, however, is often very different:

> The doorbell went. Annoyed at the interruption I went to the door. There was David a boy from up the road. 'Is Blake playing today?' ... My annoyance was short lived. Although the local children coming round to ask if Blake is coming out to play is now common, it always thrills me. I shall never take it for granted (Murray and Penman 1996).

The importance of friendships for young people with special needs is often ignored by the professionals making placement decisions, supposedly in the best interests of the child. The distress caused to young people separated from their friends on transfer from infants to junior school, or more commonly from primary to secondary education, has regularly been reported but all too often dismissed. Tim Barnes, a young man with Down's Syndrome, denied the chance to follow his friends to the local high school, made his views quite clear to the SEN Tribunal (Aspis 2000): 'The reason I want to attend the school is because it's near where I live and I will be with some of my friends from primary school. I was very happy at primary school.'

Despite the fact that the Code of Practice (DfEE 2000a) states that 'schools should make every effort to identify the ascertainable views and wishes of the child about his or her current or future education', there is currently no such duty placed on LEAs or even on the SEN Tribunal. It is hoped that the revised Code of Practice and the new

Tribunal Regulations will give more weight to the views of the child. However, this is by no means a foregone conclusion. As Morris (1998) discovered in relation to the 1989 Children Act (Department of Health and Social Security (DHSS) 1991), 'legislation has had a limited impact on the practice of consulting disabled young people about services'.

While undoubtedly acceptance and the opportunity to make and sustain friendships with local children are the prime reasons cited by families in their quest for inclusive education, they are by no means unaware of the other benefits of effective inclusion (Figure 1.2). Many comment on the positive influence of peers on their child's behaviour. In trying to keep up with their able-bodied friends, children will often push themselves to new heights or will acquire age-appropriate skills and behaviours by copying what others do, without even realising it.

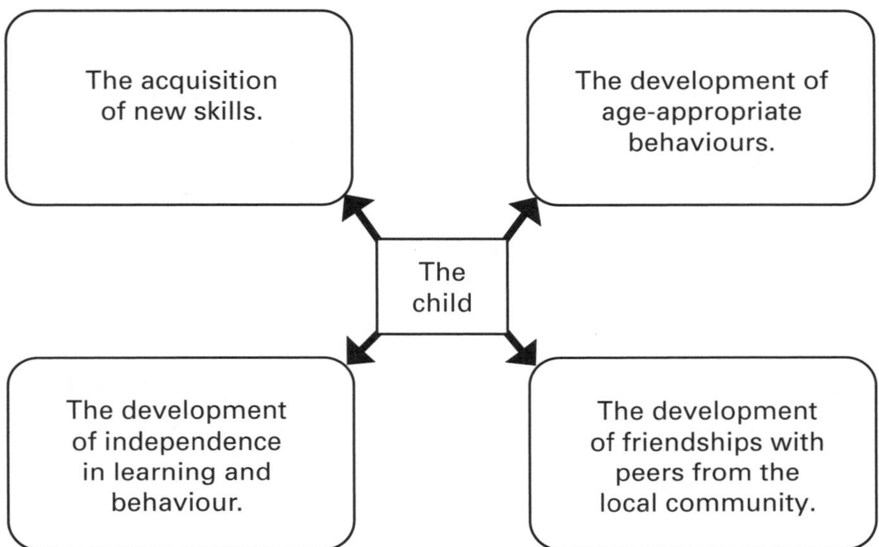

Figure 1.2 Benefits of effective inclusion

Certainly the feedback received from peers can be crucial in this process. For example, one young man quoted by Wilson and Jade (1999) noted how he had successfully moderated the behaviour of a classmate with autism: 'When we first started he used to get on my nerves because he kept on going "I'll take you for a spin" and he kept on pushing you but now he understands that if I go "No R...! I'll tell you when I want pushing", he stands there and just, like, talks to me.'

Parents of children in mainstream schools are frequently delighted by their youngster's degree of independence and confidence. This is particularly apparent when young people have moved from segregated settings. As Thomas *et al.* (1998) remarked in describing the effects of inclusion on one young man who moved out of a residential special school into a mainstream primary: 'If you talk to the coordinator you realise how much difference there is between

Tom then and Tom now he's included here. Then he was a very quiet little boy who didn't want to speak and didn't want to work and didn't like being there, and now he's screaming across the playground to his girlfriend "I love you".'

However, it is not only the children that benefit from inclusion – the parents do as well. Parents who take their child to school each day have the opportunity to work in partnership with the school and are far more likely to be involved in discussions concerning their child's educational programme. They also have the same opportunities as other local parents to enjoy the social aspects of participation in school. If families have no other children of school age, sending their disabled child to a special school can cut them off from participation in key aspects of community life and render them quite isolated. It is not only children who need friends – so do parents, and the school gate is a very good place to make them.

Chapter 2

First Steps for Parents

Choosing a school

If you are a parent or carer who has decided that you want your disabled child to be educated in a mainstream school, then this chapter is for you. There is no doubt that selecting the right school is crucial in maximising the likely success of any inclusive placement. Furthermore, you need to be clear in your own mind what you hope to gain from inclusion before you start approaching schools.

- Is it that you are committed to your child being seen as a child first and as disabled second? Do you see no need for 'special' services at all or are you looking for special services in an ordinary setting?
- Are you determined that your child should be accepted as a full member of your local community? Do you want them to take part in all the same activities as other local children or do you feel that there will be some things that they will be unable to do?
- Do you consider the most important thing to be the development of local friendship networks? Do you want your child to play with local children and be invited to parties, or do you think this is an unrealistic expectation?
- Are you concerned that your child learns to behave like other children of the same age? Do you believe that they should be expected to conform, or do you think some special allowances should made for them because of their disabilities?
- Do you think your child should be placed in a class with others of their own age and move up the school at the same rate? Or do you feel your child would be better placed with younger peers who are functioning at a similar level?
- Do you expect your child to be involved in all aspects of the ordinary class curriculum? Or, alternatively, do you feel they will need special teaching, either individually or in a small group?
- How much extra help do you believe your child needs in class to maximise their learning? Will they need a full-time helper or do you think they are better without too much help so they learn to do things for themselves?

In most areas of the country, the choice of school is left to you, the parents, even though you may have little idea what you should be looking for. Sadly, most professionals are reluctant to offer advice or guidance, despite their extensive knowledge about what goes on in individual schools. Although in theory all mainstream schools should be able to provide an effective education for any child in their neighbourhood, this is clearly not the case. So how should you go about choosing the right one?

Like the majority of parents, you probably want to see your child included in a local school where they have the opportunity to make friends with other children from your neighbourhood. Your first port of call, therefore, should always be your nearest school or the one your other children attend.

1. Make your first approaches as early as you can, preferably at least a year before your child is due to start school.
2. Ring the school and ask if you can arrange an informal visit and have a chat with the head teacher.
3. Take your partner or a friend with you so you can check out your observations later, but not your child. Remember you are vetting the school, not selling your child.
4. Try to go when the school is fully operational and make sure you get a chance to spend time watching children at work and at play.
5. Talk to children and to members of staff about the school.
6. Try not to be influenced by schoolgate gossip as it is often unreliable.
7. Be honest with the head teacher about your child, but point out their strengths as well as their weaknesses.
8. Be clear about what you want from inclusion and why you have chosen that school.
9. Take notes of your visit to help you compare schools and make choices (see Figure 2.1).
10. Don't be put off by initial reluctance by the head teacher. Most schools are vastly overstretched and may see the admission of a disabled child as yet another source of pressure. However, with patience and effort they can be won round.

School:

Date of visit:

OBSERVATION

School atmosphere:

Adult/child relationships:

Child/child relationships:

In-class support:

DISCUSSION

SEN Policy: Tick box if given copy. ☐

Name of SENCO:

No. of children with statements:

Organisation for children with SEN:

Therapy support in school:

Figure 2.1 School visit checklist

In seeking an appropriate school, you may be exposed to ignorance, prejudice and rejection, but it is important not to let this put you off. Schools vary enormously in their attitudes. For each head teacher who is hostile or negative, there will be another, often only a short distance away, who will be welcoming or at least willing to consider the proposition seriously. So don't give up – just try another school. In any case, it is always worth visiting at least two schools before making a final choice, to compare different approaches.

The key questions to ask yourself are:

- Is this a school that will welcome my child and do everything they can to make my child's educational experience a happy and successful one?

- Do I feel confident to leave my child in their care? Could I approach them openly if things seem to be going wrong?
- Does their approach to inclusion match what I want for my child?

While you are making your final decision, there are other things you can be doing to improve the chances of a successful placement.

1. Enrol your child in a local playgroup or preschool class such as 'tumble-tots'. Let them get used to being with typical children and get the children used to them.
2. Make friends with other local parents. Invite them and their children round for coffee. Help them get to know your child and be relaxed about playing with them.
3. Take your whole family to social events at your preferred school. Go to the Summer Fair and the Christmas Concert. Let the school staff and parents get to know your disabled child and feel comfortable with them.
4. Talk to your health visitor, your speech therapist, your Portage worker or anyone else you see regularly about your reasons for seeking a mainstream placement. Gain their support as you may need it in the future.
5. Where appropriate, spend time in the last few months before school teaching your child to be as independent as possible. If you can, teach them to dress themselves, go to the toilet, drink through a straw and feed themselves.

Once you have made your choice, arrange to visit the school again. But this time, take your child with you. Tell the school that you are formally applying for a place, but don't be surprised if the head teacher is not prepared to give you a response straight away. Most head teachers will want to speak to their governors or their staff before making a commitment. Others will feel the need to talk to the LEA, who will almost certainly be involved by now. So be patient – but not too patient. Remember that unless it is oversubscribed, a school must accept any child who meets their admission criteria. It is illegal for a school to reject a child purely on the basis of their disability. Despite this, some will try or will take so long in making a decision that you will give up and go elsewhere. So hang in there.

Liaising with your LEA

In most parts of England and Wales, formal assessment of children with significant disabilities will start between two and three years of age. This assessment is quite separate from any assessment your child might already have had at the child development centre or hospital, as it is carried out by the LEA under the 1996 Education Act. It may seem yet another set of hoops for you to jump through, yet it is important to play along if you think your child is going to need extra help in school. Some parents are of the opinion that it is better to avoid assessment as it stigmatises children and increases the chance of them being sent to a special school. However, this is not the common view. Most parents find a statement helpful in getting their child the help they need.

If you have not heard anything from the LEA a year before you want your child to start school, it is important to take the initiative and write to the Chief Education Officer requesting a formal assessment (see Figure 2.2). The whole process can take up to six months, so it is sensible to start early, particularly if you think you may have difficulty in getting the LEA's support for an inclusive placement. It is also useful to have thought about the school you want your child to attend before the professionals start getting involved. As Wright and Ruebain (2000) point out in their helpful book *Taking Action*, the LEA must reply to your letter, in writing, within six weeks and must agree to carry out an assessment, unless they believe that it is not 'necessary'. This decision must be based on your child's special educational needs and not on other considerations such as his or her age or any policy the LEA may have regarding preschool children.

Dear Sir or Madam,

I am writing as the parent of a child with special educational needs to ask for an assessment under section 323 of the 1996 Education Act. My child's name is .... and his/her date of birth is .... My reasons for wanting an assessment are ....
....

Figure 2.2 Letter to Chief Education Officer

Even though it is unlikely that your LEA will refuse to assess your child, they may try to delay the assessment until your child is in school or persuade you to place them in a special school or assessment unit to enable the assessment to be carried out by experts. Whatever you do, resist these suggestions. The sooner your child is assessed the more time you will have to negotiate the correct school and the appropriate package of support. If things change once your child starts school the statement can always be amended. Further, if you want an inclusive placement, try to keep your child in the mainstream. Anecdotal evidence suggests that placing a child in a special school or unit for assessment purposes will significantly reduce his or her chance of being included later.

If your LEA does refuse to assess your child, you should consider appealing to the SEN Tribunal. This appeal must be submitted within 28 days of receipt of the refusal letter from the LEA and should state why you believe your child should be assessed. If you decide to pursue this route, you can get all the advice you need from the Independent Panel for Special Educational Advice (IPSEA) or from their booklet *SENT Ahead* (Capper 1999). Once the assessment starts, there will be input from a school medical officer and an educational psychologist, neither of whom may have met you or your child before. Make sure you attend all appointments or the assessment cannot go ahead. In the case of the medical officer, it is important that you let them know of any therapists or medical staff who have been involved with your child, as it is their job to obtain reports from these people.

Although medical professionals may give useful information, it is the educational psychologist who will carry the greatest weight with the LEA and so it is important that:

- they see you more than once, so your child becomes more relaxed with them
- they see your child at home and, if possible, in a nursery or playgroup where they are with typical children, not in a clinic or hospital setting
- the assessment does not consist solely of formal tests, but also includes observation and play-based assessments
- they understand why you want a mainstream place for your child.

Ask to see a copy of the report before it goes to the LEA and let them know of any factual errors or aspects of the report you are unhappy about.

As part of the assessment you will be asked to submit your own views as to your child's needs and the provision that will be required to meet them. Make sure this includes all the things your child can do and the reasons why you feel they will do better in a mainstream school. With your advice you can include reports from anyone else who knows your child. These are not normally necessary at this stage, but they may be useful if you think you are likely to have a battle with the LEA and may need to go to the SEN Tribunal to get the mainstream provision you want.

Be prepared for quite a long wait between seeing the medical officer and educational psychologist and getting a proposed statement. In the meantime, continue making links with the school of your choice and increasing the contact between your child and their typically developing peers. Once the draft statement arrives, go through it with a fine toothcomb. Make a note of anything you are unhappy with, be it the way your child is described in Part 2, the level of in-class support offered, the therapy services to be provided or anything else. This is the point at which major changes can be made without anyone losing face. It is also your opportunity to state the school of your choice as no school will as yet have been named by the LEA.

Write back to the LEA detailing all the changes you would like made and, if you think it necessary, ask for a meeting to discuss them. Wherever possible it is always better to negotiate and try to resolve differences of opinion amicably. However, remember that if negotiations fail, your only recourse is to the SEN Tribunal. Since an appeal takes on average five months to be heard, it is wise to set a deadline for friendly discussions. Once you have got as far as you can, insist that the LEA issues a final statement.

If you are still unhappy with the final statement, write to the LEA again, detailing your concerns. Unless they are resolved speedily ask for a further meeting, but remember that you have only two months from the date of the final statement to lodge an appeal. Your LEA should issue you with a booklet on how to go about it which includes addresses of organisations who can help you. Don't try to do it all on your own. On the other hand, don't feel that you need a solicitor – most of the best sources of help are free. Whatever else you do, hold onto your belief in inclusion. Gather allies around you to give you strength and never forget that: 'inclusion begins in the love of parent for child ... Parents are the first people able to name their child's gifts and the first people able to dream of inclusion for their child' (O'Brien and Forest 1998).

Working with the school

After what might have been a long battle to obtain the mainstream place of your choice, it is tempting to sit back and heave a sigh of relief. However, this is unwise, as there is still a long way to go. As soon as you have a final statement naming the school you want, contact the head teacher and arrange another meeting. Don't worry if you are still in negotiations with your LEA about the level of support to be provided. If this is the case, the head teacher may be just the ally you need to persuade the LEA to be more generous. They may even agree to act as a witness for you at an SEN Tribunal hearing.

In any case, sit down with the head and ask the following questions:

1. When should your child start school? If the statement has been issued part-way through the school year, the head teacher may feel that your child should start straight away. Alternatively, it may be better to wait until extra support is in place, or until the start of the new term or even the new school year.

2. Which age group should they join? Generally children are best placed with others of their own age. Nevertheless, there are exceptional situations where it is in a child's best interests to move through school a year behind their peers. If they were born in the summer or have had very little preschool experience, they might be better staying in nursery for an extra year or spending two years in Reception.

3. Who should be employed as your child's support assistant? The school may already have one or several people in mind but, if so, ask to meet them and make sure you are happy with them.

Discuss whether your child would be better with one or with more than one assistant. If a new appointment is to be made, ask to be involved in the selection either by informally chatting to the candidates about your child or by being part of the interview panel.

4. What training will school staff need and who will provide it? If key staff have no knowledge of your child's particular disability, offer to find out whether there are professionals available to come into school or places they could visit. Offer to lend them any books and resources you have come across which might be helpful. But don't overdo it – remember teachers are busy people and may not have the time to read six thick books and go on a week's course before your child starts school.

5. How will your child be phased into school? Will school staff visit them at home or in their current placement to get to know them before they start school? Are they better starting on a part-time basis initially, slowly building up to full-time attendance? Would they be better going home for lunch initially or will this make fitting in even harder?

Transitions for most children with SEN are particularly important as they can affect both the child's chances of settling happily into the new school and the confidence of the staff supporting them. Even if your child has been attending a playgroup or nursery, the rules and routines of school will be very different and will take time to learn. In a Reception class, there will almost certainly be less free choice than at playgroup or nursery and more directed time. Children will probably be expected to learn to look after their own possessions, drink their milk, eat their dinner, take themselves to the toilet and change for PE with minimal help. They will also be expected to bring specified items into school on particular days.

To help them adjust, talk to your child about school. Draw pictures about what goes on and role play the various activities. If all the coat pegs at home are at adult height, think about putting a special one up at the correct height for your child and encouraging them to use it every time you come in or go out. Make sure they have a school bag that they can recognise and talk about what needs to go into it each day. Some parents find it helpful to make a picture card with everything on it for each day of the week and to get their child into the habit of packing their bag each evening, matching objects to pictures (see Figure 2.3).

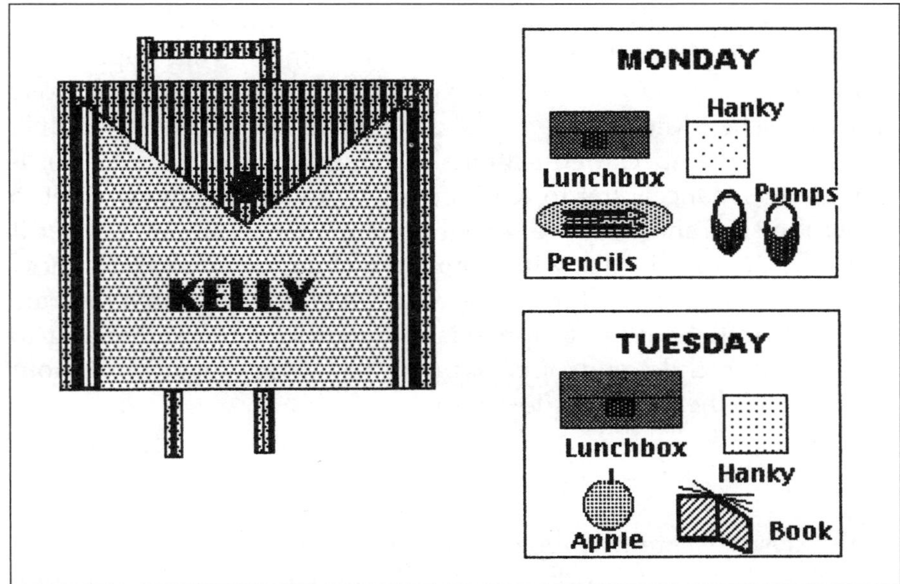

Figure 2.3 Getting ready for school

With transfers from one school phase to the next, it may be necessary to supplement the existing programme of 'taster' days, although children with special needs should always go on all the ordinary visits as well. An extra trip to the new school with their learning support assistant (LSA) or support teacher might be helpful, followed up by the drawing of a school plan and a discussion of the differences between infant and junior schools or between primary and secondary schools. Other children moving to the same school may also benefit from joining in these discussions, although they probably won't need the extra visits.

Once your child starts school, give the staff a week or so to get to know them and for your child to settle in before getting too involved. Try not to show your emotions, however worried you feel, as your child will only pick up your anxieties. Trust the teacher and do what he or she asks. Once everyone is settled and comfortable, suggest that you meet after school with the class teacher and support assistant. Try to arrange for a friend to collect your child so you have the time and space to talk freely.

At that meeting:

- Be positive about your experience of the school so far.
- Ask about the class timetable and what your child is doing.
- Ask what home–school links the teacher suggests you use.
- Find out what therapy services will be provided and how they will be incorporated into your child's programme.
- Ask about any individual or small-group work. Find out how often your child is being taken out of the classroom for special work and the reason for this.
- Ask about your child's individual education plan (IEP).

Don't worry if there is no IEP in the first few weeks as it will probably take the staff some time to get to know what approaches work best. As time goes on, try to work in partnership with your child's teacher. Make sure you talk to him or her regularly, not just the LSA or the special educational needs coordinator (SENCO). If you get the chance, offer to work in school on a regular basis. Get to know the staff and how the school operates. Generally it is better if you don't work directly with your own child, but do get to know your child's teacher and try to chat informally so you can anticipate any problems. Show you appreciate the effort staff are making to include your child and offer support wherever you can without trying to tell them how to do their job.

What to do when things go wrong

Sadly, despite careful preparation and close partnership, not all inclusive placements work smoothly. Because of this, it is important to be prepared for times when things go wrong.

Sukainah is a young lady with cerebral palsy. Her parents were called into school at the end of her first junior year following complaints from her physiotherapist who came into school weekly. Sukainah, apparently, was refusing to come to therapy sessions and when brought by her LSA refused to cooperate or threw a tantrum.

So what did her parents do to overcome the problem? First, they talked to Sukainah to get her version of what was going wrong. Then they asked for an informal meeting with the class teacher and LSA, at which it emerged that the physiotherapist always came when the class were doing practical science which Sukainah loved. In any case, she was a popular child who resented being taken out of class and away from her friends. It was agreed at that meeting that discussions would be held with the physiotherapist to see if:

- the sessions could possibly be rearranged so she missed an activity which she disliked
- she could bring a friend to the sessions with her to help with her programme
- some of the activities could be incorporated into PE lessons and her LSA trained to supervise her.

While the physiotherapist was happy to include a friend and was willing to train her LSA so she needed less withdrawal, some individual work was still required and the time of her sessions could not be altered. Her teacher, therefore, offered to change her timetable so that she only missed an occasional science lesson. Sukainah became much happier and the problem was resolved amicably.

Delroy is a young man with Asperger's Syndrome. His new high school reported that he had settled in well and was causing no concern. In contrast, his parents noticed that he was becoming increasingly withdrawn and was developing nervous tics. Whenever he had homework he got himself into a terrible state and was unable to complete the work set although it was well within his capabilities.

So what did his parents do? First they let the school know as soon as things seemed to be going wrong. They realised that frequently children say nothing in school and busy staff may, quite understandably, fail to pick up on warning signs. In this case, Delroy's parents asked for a meeting with his form tutor and shared their concerns. His tutor was surprised as there had been no complaints other than a failure to produce homework.

They explained about his autistic spectrum disorder and the anxiety it could lead to. His form teacher agreed to:

- consult the SENCO and produce a short handout for all staff on Asperger's Syndrome and ways of minimising Delroy's anxiety
- see Delroy each evening for ten minutes before he went home and go over what was expected from him for homework
- write a summary of this discussion in his planner for his parents.

This strategy worked well and Delroy began to be much happier in school. His parents also felt more confident in raising any future problems with the school.

Daniel has a variety of problems including attention deficit disorder (ADD), dyspraxia and a marked language delay. He finds it hard to concentrate in class and can lash out if he doesn't get his own way. After only a term at school, his mother, a single parent, was called in because other parents were complaining about his behaviour. She was terrified that she would be asked to take him away or put him in a special school.

So what did she do? She realised that it was important, at least initially, to be as cooperative as possible and to listen to the school. Further, she needed to make it clear from the start how important the mainstream place was to her and to Daniel. Realising that the school were genuinely at the end of their tether, she agreed that they could call in a teacher from the Behaviour Support Service or the school's educational psychologist. A behaviour support plan was set up and soon started to pay off. The head teacher agreed to talk individually to the parents who complained, explaining about Daniel's problems and what was being done to tackle them. As a consequence, the situation improved substantially and other parents started approaching Daniel's mother in a friendly way, talking about the problems they had with their children.

Terry is a sociable little boy with Down's Syndrome who lives with his widowed father. Because he was quite delayed and had missed a lot of time due to illness, it was agreed that he should spend an extra year in the nursery before starting school. However, when the time came for him to move into Reception, the head teacher stated that he was not yet ready and insisted he had a further nursery year. His father was most unhappy about this, as was Terry, because all his friends were moving up.

So what did Terry's father do? First he arranged a meeting with the head teacher to express his concerns. Sadly the head teacher was unwilling to compromise and tried to make him feel that he was being unreasonable. Next Terry's father contacted the LEA who informed him that, although they felt children should not be kept back more than a year, it was a matter for the school. On the other hand, if he was unhappy with the school, there would be a special school place readily available. In the end he approached another primary school who were happy to accept Terry into their Reception class. To avoid further problems, the LEA agreed to amend his statement to read 'Terry should move through school with peers a year younger than he is'. Fortunately, Terry settled in well and made new friends.

So what general advice might we give to parents determined to maintain their child in an inclusive placement?

1. When things start going wrong, try not to be angry with the school staff. It may not be their fault or they may not realise that there is a real problem.

2. Be open and frank with them and give them the benefit of the doubt, at least initially. To prevent conflicts between schools and families, it is important from the outset to be clear about what you are expecting from an inclusive placement.

3. Start from the premise that your child will be staying at the school. Try to get the school to accept that there is a problem that needs to be resolved, not a child who is wrongly placed.

4. Recognise when the school needs help. Suggest that it approach an appropriate outside agency and offer to support it in any way you can.

5. Don't be bullied. Hold onto what you know about your child and how their needs should be met.

6. Gather a circle of support around you. Try to find professionals or other parents who share your vision and check your actions with them.

7. If all else fails, try another mainstream school. Even the most intractable problem can often be overcome by professionals with a positive attitude towards inclusion and a commitment to making it work.

Chapter 3

First Steps for Preschool Settings

Gathering information

This chapter is aimed at anyone who works regularly in a nursery, a playgroup or any other preschool setting. Whatever your role, you are increasingly likely to be faced with the need to include a child with a disability within the groups you work with. Most children with specific medical conditions will probably have been diagnosed in early infancy. On the other hand, there will be others whose special needs have not yet been clarified. Despite the likelihood that a range of professionals may already be involved, it is important that initially you treat the family in exactly the same way as anyone else approaching your setting for the first time. Many parents of disabled children are very apprehensive on their first visit to an 'ordinary' service as they fear rejection. Sadly, many parents have been progressively deskilled and their confidence undermined by professionals who believe they know what is best and, often unwittingly, convince parents that they are not competent to make decisions about their own child.

The most important first step is to make the parent and the child feel welcome. The parent should be invited to spend some time looking around and meeting the staff and other children. A time should then be set for a longer meeting with the centre manager to discuss the child's needs. Encourage the parent to bring a partner or a friend so they can talk over what was said later. If possible, try to find a time when the child can be cared for, as it is extremely difficult for parents to talk freely when they are trying to keep their child amused. Find somewhere quiet and comfortable to meet, to put parents at their ease. Take the phone off the hook and ask colleagues to make sure you are not disturbed. To break the ice, it is probably best to start the meeting with basic factual information (see Figure 3.1). The next stage is to encourage the parent to give you a history of their child. Make a note of identified difficulties and interventions. Then ask them about the child now and make a record of the main issues raised (see Figure 3.2).

CONTACT INFORMATION

Name of child:
Date of birth:
Home address:

Name of main carer:
Telephone number(s): Home: Work:
Other carers:
Telephone numbers/addresses:

Language spoken at home:
Interpreter/friend:
Telephone number/address:

Professionals involved:

General Practitioner:
Tel:

Health visitor:
Tel:

Speech therapist:
Tel:

Physiotherapist:
Tel:

Portage worker:
Tel:

Educational psychologist:
Tel:

Social worker:
Tel:

Other(s):
Tel:

Medication:
Directions for use:

Figure 3.1 Contact information

CHILD'S HISTORY		Information to be:	
Name:	D.o.b.	shared	kept confidential
Pregnancy and birth:			
Developmental milestones:			
Medical interventions (illnesses, surgery, therapy etc.):			
Family history:			
Current situation: Family factors (siblings, care arrangements etc.):			
Strengths and interests:			
Weaknesses and particular concerns:			

Figure 3.2 Background information

Ask whether there are any professionals with useful knowledge about their child and whether they would object if you contacted them. Of the things the parent tells you, check out which they are happy for you to share with colleagues and which they would prefer you to keep confidential. It may take some time for parents to open up to you about the problems they have experienced and, even then, they are only likely to confide in you if they feel confident that you will respect their privacy. However, they need to realise that there are some things that all staff will need to be told if they are to do the best for the child.

After the initial meeting, it is useful to invite the parents back with their child for a 'taster' session. At this time you can discuss particular aspects of their care such as diet, allergies and medication. If it is clear that the child is going to require additional support or special equipment, it is important to discuss this with the parents and talk about ways of securing the required resources. It is then advisable to agree a programme of induction for the child. Some children need to be given time to get used to a new setting and new people, others will leap straight in with no difficulty. Some carers may prefer to stay at first until their child settles, while others will prefer to hand their child over directly. During this settling in period, give staff time to get to know the child without providing too much direction. Try using the Hanen approach of OWLing: Observe, Wait and Listen before jumping to any conclusions about what they can and can't do (Manolson 1992). Let the child take the lead and discover for themselves what your setting has to offer.

Even if you have not needed to secure additional help so far, it is always useful to have available information about possible sources of advice, funding or equipment. Write to as many different statutory and voluntary services as you can find and build up a resource directory, with contact numbers and the procedure by which services can be accessed. Make sure this is updated at least annually, as personnel and procedures are constantly changing. Support services, such as Portage or the service for children with a hearing impairment, may have toys or equipment they can lend you. Other aids and adaptations may be available via the hospital or social services department. In some areas there is a toy library specialising in teaching materials for children with disabilities which you or the parents should be able to join.

Having obtained the names of relevant professionals who know the child well, telephone them and invite them to come into the nursery or playgroup once the child has settled. It is much easier to talk face-to-face and they will probably appreciate the chance to see the child in the new setting. Make the visits as informal as possible and invite the parents to be there too. However, make sure you make a note of any information that is passed on. If the professionals have written recent reports, ask the parents if you can have copies for your records and again agree which aspects of any report will be shared. After a few weeks you should be in a position to hold a more formal multi-professional planning meeting, to agree with the parents the ways in which you plan to work with their child. Try to arrange this meeting at a time to suit the parents and give everyone plenty of notice as it is essential that all those actively involved with the child are able to attend.

At the planning meeting, the continuing role of outside professionals already involved can be agreed and coordinated with what you are offering. Some parents like to combine sessions in a local nursery or playgroup with specialist sessions at the child development centre or clinic. Others will prefer to use only 'ordinary' services, supplemented by therapy at home or in the nursery. Where key professionals are not yet involved with the child, the planning meeting can be used to gain parental agreement for a referral either from you or via another agency such as the family GP. Make sure the parents understand what, if anything, their role is in this process and whether it will be necessary for them to take their child to a hospital or clinic to be seen.

Finally, there will need to be some agreement with the LEA about the assessment process. Since all the children referred to in this book will have significant and long-term needs, they will all, eventually, require the protection of a Statement of Special Educational Need. In some cases, formal assessment will already have started and you may well be expected to contribute. In others, it will be up to you to alert the LEA to the child's needs and trigger the process once you have gathered the requisite information. Whichever is the case, it is your responsibility to make sure that the parents are fully aware of what is happening and feel supported as they participate in a potentially stressful procedure.

Developing a partnership with parents

Once the child has settled into your early years setting, a dialogue should be established between nursery and parents. To aid this process, it is helpful to identify a key worker who will be parents' first point of contact and who will liaise with both nursery staff and outside professionals. If parents are at work or share the child's care with a grandparent or childminder, it may be a good idea to operate a diary system, allowing the parents to contribute to discussions regarding the child and to be kept informed of progress or problems. A bilingual member of staff or a visiting member of the local community might be useful in translating key comments where parents are using English as an additional language. Whatever the situation, it is essential that parents feel involved and are given the opportunity to come into the nursery at regular intervals and at a time that fits in with their other commitments. In some cases, evening meetings or home visits may be required to guarantee participation.

As Sue Roffey (1999) notes 'Parental involvement, responsibility and inclusion in both decision making and service delivery is an

integral part of all the legislation and guidance on SEN'. Maintaining parental responsibility and rights is also stressed in the Children Act 1989 (DHSS 1991). Under the Act, both parents have rights and responsibilities regarding the child, even if they are not living together, as long as they were married when the child was born. Thus both must be consulted when key decisions, such as the choice of a mainstream as opposed to a special school, are made.

Where children are being 'looked after' by the local authority, either with foster parents or in a children's home, communication can be even more problematic. However, since it is the local authority who hold parental responsibility, it is essential that the child's social worker is invited to all significant meetings. On a day-to-day basis, it is helpful for the foster parent or a key worker from the children's home to be involved in informal discussions, although with frequent changes of staff the latter can be difficult to achieve in all cases.

The whole area of disability is a very sensitive one and so careful thought must be given to the messages conveyed to parents. While many will have been given factual information about their child's medical condition, much of the detail may have been forgotten or misinterpreted because of the strong emotions generated by the diagnosis. Some parents would rather not accept that their child will definitely have long-term special needs and prefer to wait and see. Others, quite rightly, will have rejected a very negative prognosis and be keen to work productively to ensure the best possible outcome for their child. Cultural factors may also be of relevance here, as disability may bring shame on the family or be attributed to some failing on the parents' part, leading to denial.

In talking to parents about their child, it is important to stress the positives and the gains made, albeit from a low base. Always celebrate successes publicly, but try to keep problems to more private discussions away from other parents. Before sharing concerns with parents, it is essential to observe the child for a reasonable period of time and in a range of settings to establish the facts. Sharing concerns with colleagues is also important, as children can react quite differently with different people. Notes made at the time, albeit on a sheet of paper stuck to the wall or a handy notebook, are more useful than carefully produced reports written up at the end of the day or just before a review. When you are busy it is easy to forget or simplify key elements of the child's behaviour, or lose sight of what else was going on at the time to trigger the particular incident.

Think carefully about your language. Some outdated terms such as 'retarded', 'subnormal' or 'Mongol', while once in common use, are now seen as offensive and should never be used. Others such as 'developmental delay' or 'withdrawn', which seem quite harmless, may be misinterpreted by anxious parents. In describing a child, try to avoid generalisations. Instead, describe the child's behaviour as precisely as you can and look for the positives:

- Instead of saying 'He's really aggressive with other children' say 'He is a bit over-enthusiastic in greeting other children and tries to cuddle them really hard, which unfortunately most of them don't like'.
- Instead of 'She never settles to anything' you could say 'She likes to have a go at everything we are doing, although she only spends two or three minutes at any one activity'.

If parents are facing problems within the family, particular care may be needed to avoid attributing inappropriate or challenging behaviours to poor parenting. Behaviour needs to be seen in context and there may be a variety of factors, both within the nursery and outside, that are contributing to the problem. Families under stress may need a great deal of help, not only in accepting their child's difficulties but also in working with professionals who can be seen as threatening or patronising. Hospital or clinic appointments may be missed because of difficulties with transport or child care, or just a fear of being talked down to. In such cases, arranging for someone the parent trusts to accompany them or, even better, persuading the professionals to see the child in the nursery, can help break down barriers.

Parents of children with SEN may be carrying a burden of anger, fear or guilt. They may need a great deal of time and reassurance to be able to share their hopes and worries with you. However, parents who establish a positive and supportive relationship with nursery or playgroup staff are generally more able to work productively with other professionals to achieve what they believe is in the best interests of their child. In working with parents of children with SEN it is important to:

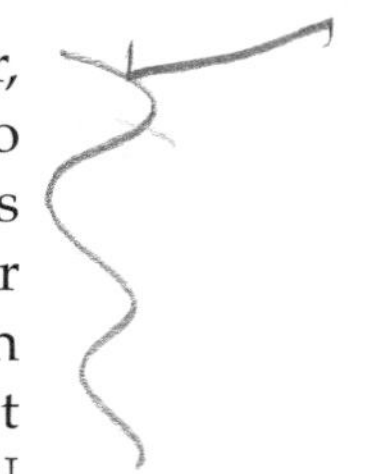

- make time for them
- be a good listener
- understand how they are feeling
- respect their point of view
- try not to blame them for any difficulties
- share information about their child
- give advice sensitively
- build trust.

When children with significant difficulties in one or more
their development enter a preschool setting, they are likel
accompanied by information about their SEN from a va
sources. In interpreting this information, don't forget that:

- children may react quite differently in a clinic as opp nursery situation
- medical diagnoses and labels tell us very little about i children
- young children change very rapidly.

It is therefore essential for you to carry out your own assessment of the child before planning any intervention strategy or setting learning goals. Wherever possible, try to stand back and observe the child taking part in ordinary activities. Where appropriate, supplement your observations with relevant assessment schedules or checklists that can help you to ask the right questions.

The *Early Learning Goals* (Qualifications and Curriculum Authority (QCA) 2000) stress the need for every child to engage in 'activities that promote emotional, moral and spiritual development alongside intellectual development'. For children with special needs, it is particularly important that preschooling allows them to gain in confidence, to form good relationships with adults and peers, to gain in independence and to show interest, excitement and the motivation to learn. In assessing the child's skills in these areas, it is necessary to observe them in a range of different situations. Some children feel more confident in a structured setting in which there are clear rules and routines. Others operate better when they can move, at will, between activities. Some children prefer a quiet tranquil environment where they feel safe, others need the opportunity to roar around and let off steam.

Even at nursery level, some children have relatively advanced social skills and are able to work cooperatively. Others are still quite egocentric and find it hard to share or take turns. Those who have had little experience of other children may, initially, prefer the company of adults and need encouragement to play alongside their peers. Others will take delight in large groups where there is a wide choice of playmates. For children with special needs, the ability to seek help from adults or other children is extremely valuable, but may not be exercised where a parent has always been at hand to anticipate and resolve difficulties. Presenting the child with a problem and then observing how they deal with it can be a very informative strategy and may reveal skills not usually employed.

Dressing, feeding and toilet training are all important if the young child is to function independently. Yet these skills are often poorly developed in many children when they first start at nursery or playgroup. This could be because of a physical difficulty or medical condition that affects muscular control. It could be part of a general delay and reflect the child's awareness of their own body. Alternatively, it may be due to lack of practice or low expectations at home. Here particular sensitivity may be required to avoid the parent feeling they are being blamed. Above all else, it is important to gain their support, as intervention is only likely to succeed if programmes implemented in school are backed up at home.

Marina was in nappies when she started at nursery and her mother reported that she was not yet ready to be toilet trained. However, her key worker noticed that she pulled at her nappy whenever she had wet or soiled herself and said 'poo'. She also realised that Marina could go for up to two hours with a dry nappy. She shared these observations with Marina's mother who agreed that the time might now be right to start a toilet training programme.

As the Early Learning Goals specify, young children need 'to communicate thoughts, feelings and ideas to an adult or to each other'. For many children, the ability to use or understand the spoken word may be limited because of a hearing loss, difficulties in processing language or in producing speech sounds. Nevertheless they will, almost invariably, have some form of communication and it is your job to learn their language.

Shazad was a little boy who made a range of noises but had no recognisable words in English or Punjabi, his first language. Despite this, he had no difficulty in making his wishes known. If he wanted something, he would look at it and point, making an assertive noise. If the other person got it wrong, he would take them by the hand towards the object and point again until the penny dropped.

Assessing the child's ability to make sense of the world and solve problems for themselves can prove highly instructive. Children considered to have very significant learning difficulties may prove themselves adept at reaching toys in a high cupboard or escaping through locked doors. Others with little useful sight can show surprising skill in constructing models with materials such as Duplo or Sticklebricks. Left to themselves to explore and experiment, children with marked disabilities can surprise themselves and those around them. On the other hand, this knowledge can be lost if, from the onset, staff stay close to the child and direct their activities. Similarly, other children can stifle exploration and discovery by taking control and 'looking after' a child with special needs.

Chan was a friendly but passive boy who was happy to let other children treat him like a baby. In the sand tray they would help him to make sand pies, filling the bucket for him and guiding his hand to turn the pie out. However, on one occasion the other children were kept away and he was encouraged to play in the sand by himself. After a short while, he discovered that he could make the sandmill spin by pouring sand into the top and this gave him evident enjoyment.

Every child should develop the ability 'to move with confidence, imagination and in safety, to move with control and coordination and to show awareness of space, of themselves and of others' (QCA 2000). To facilitate this process, you will need to find out about his or her level of independent mobility and to examine the equipment and activities on offer to see how they might be modified. Just because a child has a medical condition or physical disability that restricts their movement, it does not mean that they are unable to get around the nursery or take part in active games.

Sadia has hydrocephalus and spina bifida and is paralysed from the waist down. Despite her physical limitations, she can shuffle around the floor at speed and she gains considerable pleasure from the outdoor slide and swings, as long as there is someone to put her on and take her down.

For many children with significant disabilities, the area of creative play is one in which they can excel and gain real pleasure. There should be no reason why every child should not have the opportunity to experiment with paint and clay and join in musical games. Colour, texture, sound, taste, vibration and reflection can all be used to help the child use all their senses. Their responses to varied experiences can provide valuable insights into ways in which their environment might be structured to maximise learning opportunities.

Grant is registered deaf and blind, yet he responds positively to music, humming to himself and smiling with real enjoyment. If a friend holds his hand and helps him with the actions, he will join in singing games with evident pleasure. He also becomes quite animated when surrounded by bright lights and moving colours. Using finger paints, he has made colourful patterns on paper, enjoying the feel of the paint on his fingers.

Meeting children's learning needs

However marked the child's difficulties, never forget that he or she is a child first and foremost, with just the same needs as all other children. If you start with ensuring that they feel safe, comfortable and happy you will not go far wrong. The next stage is to give them opportunities to experience the range of activities available in the nursery or playgroup, interact naturally with other children and receive praise for their achievements. Try to follow the advice of the Hanen programme (Manolson 1992):

- Don't do all the talking.
- Don't offer help when it's not needed.
- Don't direct the show.
- Don't interrupt the child's play.
- Don't get in the way of early friendships.
- Don't assume you know what the child wants.

If children have already been introduced to a signing system such as 'Makaton' (MVDP [Makaton Vocabulary Development Project] 2000) it would be advisable to arrange training for the key worker and, ideally, for the rest of your staff. For some children, sign may be their first language so it is important that as many people as possible are able to understand and use a basic repertoire of appropriate signs. They are really quite easy to learn and other children will enjoy learning them as well.

Following on from your assessment and discussions with the parents and involved professionals, it should be possible to set a series of learning goals for the child. Ideally these should focus on developing all the skills shown in Figure 3.3.

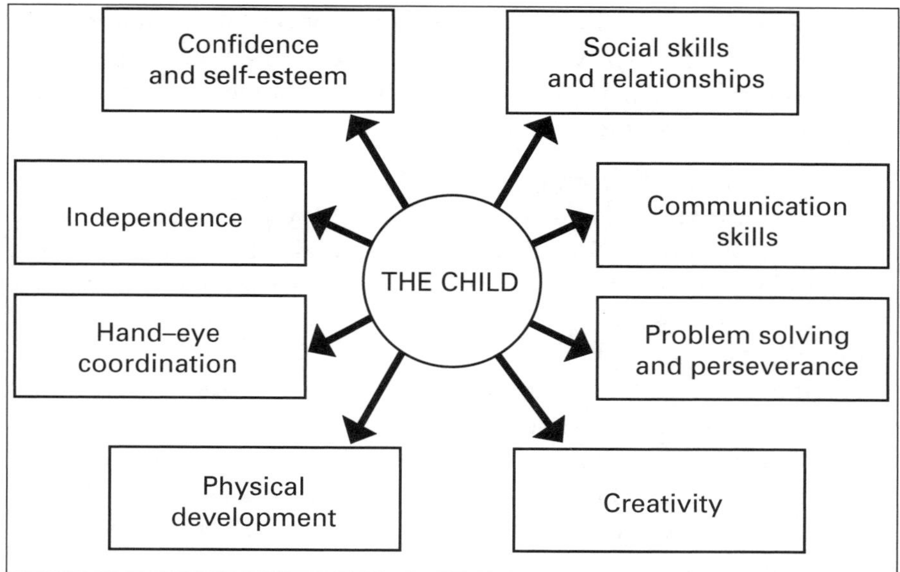

Figure 3.3 Developing skills

Opportunities should be created to allow goals to be achieved by active participation in normal nursery activities. To enable the child to take a full part, it may be necessary:

- to provide special equipment or adapt what is already available
- to create a quiet area where distractions are kept to a minimum for the child who becomes distressed by too much noise or movement around them
- to break down certain activities into smaller units, with a gap between, for the child who finds it hard to concentrate for long.
- to model new skills and allow the child to practise them before joining the larger group
- to accompany verbal instructions with Makaton signs or gestures
- to pair children up for some tasks so that everyone has a supportive friend to help them out when they have difficulties.

Where children are presenting with inappropriate behaviours, it is important that these do not become the focus of attention and result in the child being prevented from joining in. Make every effort to discover what is triggering the behaviour and what is causing it to recur:

- Is the child being egged on by others?
- Are they seeking adult attention by deliberate naughtiness?
- Are they angry or frustrated because of their inability to do the same as their peers?
- Are they confused or uncertain about what is expected of them?
- Is their behaviour typical of a younger child but in line with their general development?

Before intervening, it is vital that your concerns are shared with the parents and their views sought. Unless they, and any other carers, support you, it is unlikely that a behaviour management programme will be successful.

- If you believe other children are the cause of the problem help them to understand the consequences of their actions. Even very young children can begin to learn about disability and to value others, whatever their differences. Include books in your book corner that illustrate positive images of children with different disabilities.
- If children are attention seeking, reward appropriate behaviours and ignore silliness. Some children with disabilities have become used to getting a lot of adult attention in hospital or at home because of their ill health or therapy needs. Others are not used to sharing attention with other children, so need time to adjust to new expectations.
- Where children are clearly frustrated, take time to review your arrangements and see if they can be helped to gain more success or participate more fully in nursery life. Never insist that a child is withdrawn for special work when they would clearly prefer to remain with their friends. Work hard at listening to what they are trying to tell you, particularly when they have not yet developed recognisable speech.
- If the child seems confused or uncertain, make sure everyone is in agreement as to how they should be treated and allow no special favours. Involve the family and other carers in your planning as different expectations at home and in school can cause the child real difficulties. Make sure you are very clear about the rules and what you expect, and check that the child has understood you.
- Finally, if the problem is one of immaturity, it may be necessary to make some allowances and explain to the other children why the disabled child cannot yet do everything they can. Keep your expectations high and help the child work towards age-appropriate behaviour. It may also be necessary to help the parents to let their child grow up and begin to take more risks. For some, who still see their child as a precious baby who needs all their care and protection, this can take time.

While the aim should be to maximise the child's participation in mainstream activities, there may be occasions when this is not possible or desirable. Some children get very distressed by noisy games with other children running round them. They may need to be withdrawn to a quiet area to calm down. Others may become very tired towards the end of the day and need a rest.

Some children can be fully engaged for the first part of an activity and then lose interest when their concentration begins to lapse. However, don't jump to conclusions about a child's ability to take part. Start each day afresh and always let them try, only removing them when they are becoming distressed or are upsetting others. You may be surprised to see how their skills improve or their tolerance increases each time they are exposed to the same set of circumstances.

Where withdrawal is indicated, use the time productively to work on specific areas of development which are difficult to address within the ordinary curriculum. There may be exercises recommended by a therapist to strengthen muscles or improve mobility which require special equipment or a degree of privacy. There may be structured language activities, suggested by the speech therapist, which need to be carried out in a distraction-free setting without an inquisitive audience. Whenever possible include at least one other child in these sessions and keep them short and focused. Remember your long-term aim is inclusion, so try to get them back in the swing of things as soon as you can.

Chapter 4

First Steps for Primary Schools

Welcoming diversity

This chapter is written for you if you are a head teacher or a member of the senior management team (SMT) in a maintained primary school. Whether you work in a tiny rural school, with one or two classes covering the full primary range, or in a large inner-city primary, with three or four parallel classes in each year group, the issues are just the same although the practicalities may be very different.

> An educationally inclusive school is one in which the teaching and learning, achievements, attitudes and well-being of every young person matter. Effective schools are educationally inclusive schools. This shows, not only in their performance, but also in their ethos and their willingness to offer new opportunities to pupils who may have experienced previous difficulties. This does not mean treating all pupils the same way. Rather it involves taking account of pupils' varied life experiences and needs (Office for Standards in Education (OFSTED) 2000).

As OFSTED note in their guidance for school inspectors (OFSTED 2000) effective schools:

- constantly monitor and evaluate the progress each pupil makes
- identify any pupils who may be missing out or feeling in some way apart
- promote tolerance and understanding in a diverse society.

It is very encouraging to see OFSTED stressing the need for schools to cater equally for all their pupils, while at the same time holding fast to the belief that all schools should achieve high standards. As Priscilla Alderson, in her account of Cleves Primary School (Alderson 1999) comments, the government's expectation that all schools should achieve the best possible results in tests and exams could appear to conflict with the policy of including children of all types and abilities in the mainstream. However, experience has shown that this need not necessarily be the case.

So how can you, in your particular circumstances, achieve an inclusive ethos without sacrificing achievement and losing your hard-earned position in the league tables? Some answers can be found in the *Index for Inclusion* (Booth *et al.* 2000) sent to all maintained schools by the DfEE in 2000. This helpful document talks about:

- creating inclusive cultures
- producing inclusive policies
- evolving inclusive practices.

Instead of using the term 'special educational needs' the authors talk about 'barriers to learning and participation' which can affect any child within the school system. In their view, these barriers arise not from within individuals, but in the interaction between students and their contexts. Just as the McPherson Report (1999) talked about institutional racism, there exist inbuilt practices and attitudes in schools which discriminate against students with disabilities. If your school is to become more inclusive, these prejudices need to be challenged, although change may be slow and painful. Above all, proposals for promoting inclusion need to be integrated into your existing school development plan and ongoing priorities.

In creating an inclusive culture, it is important that everyone is made to feel welcome be they visitors, staff or students. Cleves Primary School is fully accessible for disabled people and has a school foyer where children's art work is displayed. There is a ball pool for young visitors and a comfortable seating area where the parent and toddler group meet most mornings. But not all primary schools are like this. Take a walk around your school and imagine you are seeing it for the first time. Would you want to send your child there?

Feelings of alienation may also be felt by new pupils or new staff if there is no clear induction programme and they are not actively welcomed into school. Some schools operate a 'buddy' system for new arrivals. Others hold a welcome assembly where new children and staff are encouraged to tell other people something about themselves. Many schools have photographs of all staff members in the entrance hall and these are just as useful for new staff as they are for visitors. There is nothing more embarrassing than confusing the deputy head with the caretaker, but mistakes such as this are easily made when you are new.

In the inclusive school, students help each other and collaborative working is encouraged. Bullying and name calling are dealt with effectively and students feel that they will be listened to and believed if they report concerns. This is particularly important for disabled students who may find it difficult to articulate their worries and need friends who can support them in seeking adult help. Sadly, in some schools, bullying is just as rife in the staffroom as it is in the playground. Staff who feel unsafe or insecure cannot meet the needs of the children they are employed to support and teach.

All staff should feel valued equally, whether they are the school superintendent, the part-time cleaner, the lunchtime supervisor, the parent governor, the supply teacher or the newly qualified teacher (NQT). Every member of the school community should be treated with respect. Sit in the staffroom one lunchtime and listen to the way in which your staff talk about absent colleagues, the children they teach or their parents. You will learn a lot about staff attitudes and prejudices. Try to foster collaboration between staff as well as between children, and take a hard look at interactions between school and parents. The whole ethos of a school can be changed by a major review of written communications between school and home. Make your letters sent to children's homes easy to read, attractive to look at and fun. Involve the children. If they have coloured in the invitation to the school open day, they are more likely to make sure their parents read it and come, instead of leaving it screwed up at the bottom of their school bag.

High expectations of all students are the key to successful inclusive practice. Do your staff accept that they can break down barriers to learning for individual students or do they feel that any difficulties are intractable and lie within the pupils themselves? Everyone, whatever their disability, must feel that they can achieve and that their achievements will be celebrated. Ask yourself who gets the accolades and the prizes in your school?

The way in which children view themselves and each other is another good performance indicator. If you group children by ability for some subjects, do you know how your pupils and their parents feel about this? Do your low achievers believe that they will get more help and cope better in small groups, or do they feel a sense of failure and believe they have been written off? What about the Literacy Hour? Despite the fact that the National Literacy Strategy was designed to include all learners (Berger and Gross 1999), many schools still withdraw students with special needs for individual tuition. How do they feel about this? Do they enjoy the extra attention or do they feel left out?

For many primary schools, the use of circle time (Curry and Broomfield 1994) has been invaluable in helping children respect and care for each other. In some places this work has been developed further to enable children with difficulties to be helped by a 'Circle of Friends' (Wilson and Newton 1999) who develop action plans to help them cope better. Are you using approaches such as these in your school or are they seen as less important than boosting next year's standard assessment tasks (SATs) results?

Working together as a whole school

Frank McAneny (personal communication), the principal of an elementary school in the USA, recently described how inclusion became a reality in his school: 'It was a planned process that has been part of our program for eight years. It included a great deal of teacher training that continued to be part of our program. We started out small with a few interested teachers and presently have involved all our teachers in opportunities for inclusion.'

He stresses the importance of getting all staff on board, albeit gradually, and of offering them the support they need. In his school, staff attend early morning staff meetings during which teachers are able to exchange ideas regarding approaches already attempted to allow other teachers to see the possibilities in their own classrooms. As he says: 'Planning is the key ... where are we now ... where can we be in two months ... in four months ... this time next year? It works and before you know it you are beyond where you thought you could be.'

At Cleves Primary School, teamwork is central to successful inclusion. Staff are grouped into teams of up to 12 staff, responsible for around 120 children. Each team comprises four base teachers, one curriculum support teacher and six or seven LSAs. All the teaching staff work at different times with all the children, while LSAs work as links rather than individual supporters. The shared expertise of the team enables them to cover a very wide curriculum for children of all abilities. Dividing up the preparation and teaching time among the staff means that each session can have more staff time and attention than would be the case if only one teacher covered the whole curriculum for their teaching group. While not all schools will want to adopt this approach, team teaching has undoubted benefits for both staff and pupils.

Team teaching:

- enables each child to benefit from the expertise of more than one teacher
- gives teachers the chance to develop a specialism
- enables the school to offer a wider curriculum
- provides a model of sharing and cooperation for pupils to follow
- prevents total reliance on one adult
- encourages pupils to become more independent
- reduces stress and boosts confidence.

Involving all members of the school community in the development of inclusive practices is a process advocated strongly by the authors of the *Index for Inclusion* (Booth *et al.* 2000). As they state in the Introduction, it encourages the whole school to take ownership of the process of inclusive school development. This step is perhaps the most critical. If changes introduced as a result of working with the index are to be sustainable, then they need to be experienced as improvements to teaching and learning by staff and students alike. They need to become part of the school culture.

However enthusiastic you might be as a head teacher to introduce more inclusive practices in your school, it is vital that you have the support of your staff and your governors, even if this means going more slowly than you might otherwise prefer. Before introducing a powerful tool such as the *Index for Inclusion*, you need to ensure that there is a climate that fosters effective communication and the development of trust.

In the teaching profession, teamwork makes good sense, particularly at primary level. The typical primary teacher is expected to plan, teach and assess all subjects of the curriculum, organise and supervise extra-curricular activities and meet the emotional, physical, social and intellectual needs of up to 45 students. All this with little if any in-class support, secretarial assistance or free time. As Reif and Heimburge (1996) point out, teaching is a lonely profession. Primary teachers are in their classrooms for up to six hours a day, with little time to communicate and exchange ideas or frustrations with other adults. For many teachers, team teaching has become a way to meet the challenges in a productive way.

To ensure that teams work effectively from the start it is important that all potential members believe that working in a team will make their teaching more effective and offer benefits to themselves, their colleagues and their pupils. Teams need to be built from members with complementary skills, teaching styles and temperaments. Team members need:

- flexibility
- good communication skills
- professionalism
- the desire to work with others
- a sense of humour
- respect for other people's opinions.

If you, as a school manager, wish your staff to develop effective team-working it is essential that you provide the necessary supports. They will need:

- time in which to plan and develop their ideas
- space to meet and store team resources
- opportunities to work together, regroup pupils and reorganise teaching areas
- team support in the form of welfare or clerical assistance
- recognition by managers and governors of the benefits of teamwork.

When we look at the development of more inclusive schools, it is clear that effective working involves not only collaboration between members of the school community, but also cooperative working with a whole range of outside professionals. For many students with significant difficulties, their educational experience includes regular input from a whole range of professionals (see Figure 4.1) Traditionally, many of these services were offered at a clinic or on a withdrawal basis within the school. Now, as schools become more inclusive, support personnel are increasingly working in classrooms alongside teachers. For this input to be effective it is essential that it is integrated into the child's programme and that class teacher and support staff work closely together. Where this collaboration is effectively planned and managed, class teachers feel supported and are far more willing to go that extra mile in meeting the needs of individual students.

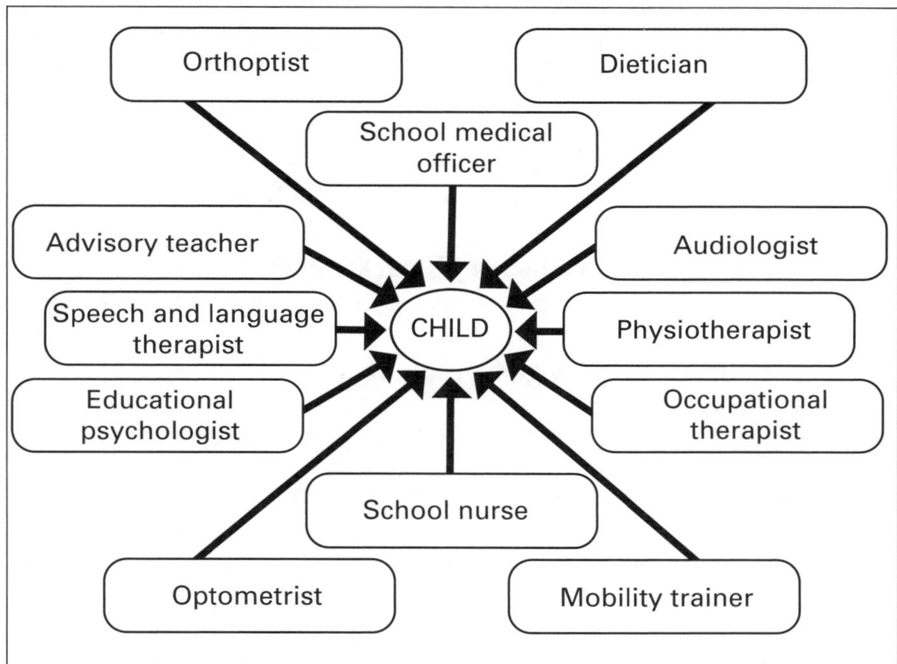

Figure 4.1 Professional links

Accessing the curriculum

'At the heart of any debate on the curriculum and its influence upon inclusion, must be an understanding of what it is we expect to achieve through its implementation' (Rose 1998). The curriculum of a school cannot be viewed as an end in itself, but merely as a vehicle for learning. Schools that aim to provide a climate for inclusion need to offer a curriculum which serves to transmit a body of knowledge and values applicable to all while, at the same time, recognising the individuality of each pupil.

Teachers must understand not only the content of the curriculum they are providing, but also the way in which different pupils learn, and the variety of strategies they might use to deliver the curriculum to all their pupils. While in some aspects, such as the National Literacy and Numeracy Strategies, both curricular content and preferred teaching methods are laid down by government edict, there is still enormous scope for the resourceful teacher to determine the breadth, structure and delivery of their classroom curriculum.

Authors such as Evans (1997) are clear that successful inclusive practice will not be achieved unless every teacher accepts full responsibility for the learning of each and every pupil in their class. The whole school community needs to review the curriculum on a regular basis, at both a philosophical and a practical level. Sadly the recent emphasis on core skills has meant that many schools have lost sight of the original assertion that the curriculum should be broad and balanced. Establishing a balance, particularly for pupils with SEN, may mean schools focusing far more than they do at present on aspects outside the core and foundation subjects.

Take a look at your own school curriculum. Do you expect staff to concentrate on raising academic achievement above all else or do you encourage them to offer a lot more? Write a list of all the extra activities you offer outside the National Curriculum.

- Do you find time to teach thinking skills?
- Can pupils learn French or Spanish, British Sign Language or Bengali?
- Does each day start or finish with circle time?
- Can children sit on a school council or get involved in peer mediation?
- Do your students grow their own vegetables, keep chickens or help run a school farm?
- Can they learn Scottish dancing, chess or canoeing?

One of the big questions facing those responsible for providing an appropriate educational experience for young people with significant disabilities is the extent to which they should participate in the same activities as their peers. A real tension exists between the desire to include the child in mainstream learning experiences and the often mistaken belief that they will be happier and achieve better outcomes when modified or specialised programmes of study are offered.

For many children with SEN there is little choice, as the class teacher has few resources to call upon and limited opportunity to provide small-group or individual teaching. On the other hand, where pupils have statements and are provided with additional support from an LSA or support teacher, more options are available. However, where specialised approaches are being considered, it is important to be clear that they are for the benefit of the child, not just a way to get the class teacher off the hook.

Over the years, many teachers have become very proficient in the art of differentiation and adaptation of teaching methods and materials. However, in some schools, such practices have been used to increase segregation instead of promoting inclusion. The substitution of different and less demanding tasks, often delivered on a one-to-one basis by an unqualified assistant or in a withdrawal group, can prevent participation rather than promoting it.

Whereas most proponents of inclusive education would encourage schools to keep children in mixed ability settings for as much of the time as possible, schools are under increasing pressure to stream, set or group by ability within the classroom. If you have reached the decision that overall such approaches are best for your school, there is still a lot you can do to foster inclusion. First of all, think about the learning environment that provides the best opportunity for the individual child. Spending most of their time in a special needs group with peers who have a poor attitude to learning might not best serve their interests. Instead they may do far better with more able or better motivated peers.

Think carefully about all the learning opportunities available in the school day and beyond. Make sure that the child with significant difficulties is able to access as many of these as possible. Where children are bussed in from outside your normal catchment area, try to ensure that their day is not cut short and that they have access to breakfast clubs and after-school activities. Encourage therapists or outreach teachers to come into school and work alongside your staff in the classroom. Liaise with your local hospital or clinic to minimise the amount of time the child needs to be out of school.

Encourage anxious parents to allow their child to participate in school trips or weekends away. Never forget that for all children, learning is as much about the acquisition of social skills, age-appropriate behaviour and independence as it is about accessing the National Curriculum. This is particularly so for a child with special needs and is best achieved by giving them maximum access to the day-to-day life of the school. It is also about taking certain calculated risks. A disabled child who is continually watched and protected from possible dangers will never learn to face challenges and will grow up to be fearful and dependent on adults. By standing back and allowing the child to interact with peers and cope with difficulties, you will be equipping them with vital life skills.

In designing an inclusive timetable for an individual child, it is often helpful to use the clover leaf model (see Figure 4.2). Start with the normal class curriculum and consider where the child could possibly cope without extra support. Encourage the class teacher to take responsibility for assembly, PE or story time, allowing the LSA to use the time saved for preparation and planning of future lessons. Each term, expand the range of activities the child can cope with independently. Teach them to ask for help when they need it and to approach friends or their class teacher. Over time, the confidence and skills of the class teacher will increase and peers will begin to see the disabled child as an ordinary member of the class.

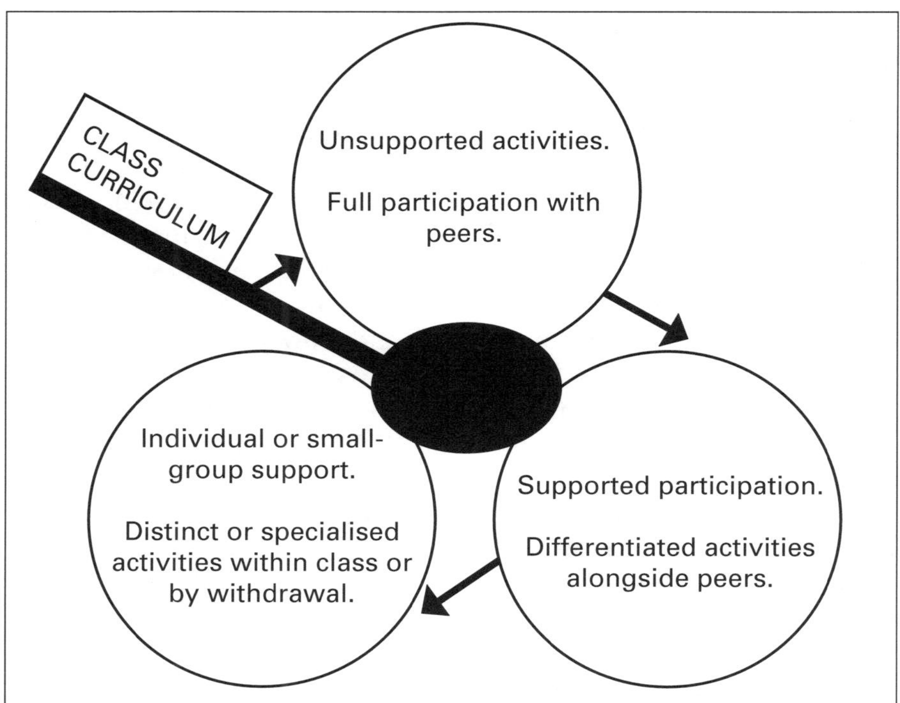

Figure 4.2 The clover leaf model

All disabled children, however great their needs, should be able to participate in some class activities without individual support. Yet, for many, this will not be realistic for much of the school day. Some children will need a high level of physical support; others will need help in remaining on task or in understanding what they are expected to do. The aim should be to maximise the participation of the child in typical activities alongside their peers and to steadily increase their independence. Nevertheless, for children with high level support needs, there are likely to be times when access to the class curriculum is not possible to achieve. While individual working or withdrawal should never be the first option, there will undoubtedly be times when such an approach best meets the needs of the child and the class.

Managing support staff

In looking at curriculum access for children with significant needs, it is important to pay particular attention to the way in which support staff are used. As Rose (1998) comments: 'The use of classroom support to enable pupils with special educational needs to access mainstream lessons has been a traditional route by which the inclusion of pupils has been achieved, yet this is an area fraught with possible dangers.'

Where inappropriately deployed, LSAs can:

- take the responsibility for managing the child away from the class teacher
- reduce the quality of teaching the child receives
- isolate the child from the class curriculum by focusing on individual programmes
- isolate the child from the peer group
- single the child out and stigmatise them
- create a culture of adult dependency.

Increasingly teachers and the government are seeing teaching assistants as a way of taking pressure off overworked teachers and overcoming growing teacher shortages. However, teaching assistants themselves (Shaw 2001) are clear that they are there for the child. Supporters see themselves as making a distinct contribution to schools and view their work as complementary to that of the teacher. Their hope is that in the near future they will be accepted and valued as equal members of the inclusion team, with a pay and career structure that reflects their unique contribution.

In managing a primary school which is adopting a more inclusive philosophy, you will undoubtedly be responsible for deploying one or more teaching assistants. The way in which they are recruited and employed will depend a great deal on the nature of your school. In planning an appropriate package of support for an individual child, many factors need to be taken into consideration.

- How are relevant classes organised and children grouped?
- Are there other children with similar or very different needs?
- Are other adults available to offer support?
- What type of support does each individual child need and want?
- What type of support does each teacher need and want?
- Are particular skills and competencies required by supporters?
- Is each individual child best supported by one person or could jobs be shared?

At one end of the continuum are those settings in which all classes operate on a mixed ability model with children only occasionally grouped by attainment or aptitude. Whole-class teaching is heavily differentiated so that all students can ideally participate and succeed. Collaborative working is encouraged between staff and students. In such schools, support workers tend to work in partnership with teachers rather than with named pupils. They rarely withdraw students, except in an emergency, and their task is to enable all students to participate in a shared curriculum.

This approach is the one favoured by the Cleves Primary School (Alderson 1999) where each wing has six learning support staff. As they say: 'Their work is mainly in curriculum support for children with special needs, although all the children work with all the staff on the wing. We wanted to get away from the idea that any child needs one to one support.'

An integrated approach can work well if:

- Class teachers are fully committed to inclusion and are prepared to put in the extra effort required to differentiate their lessons for all students.
- Support staff are skilled and confident in teamworking across the curriculum.
- Staff teams are built up over time and are maintained from one year to the next.
- Class teachers and support staff are given adequate time to plan their work and develop appropriate resources.

In marked contrast is the school where children are grouped for most of their school day on the basis of their ability or attainment. They may be in parallel classes catering for the more and the less able. Alternatively they may be set across several age groups for literacy and/or numeracy. Such approaches are becoming increasingly common at primary level, even within Key Stage 1. Even where schools reject these approaches in favour of mixed ability classes, ability grouping is still the norm for core subjects in an increasing number of schools. In these settings, children with additional needs tend to be taught with the least able. Support staff will generally be used to work with this group either within the classroom or on a withdrawal basis.

Where this type of support works well:

- Children in the special needs group also have opportunities to work with the whole class, with more able peers and directly with the class teacher.
- Activities are set by the teacher, ideally in consultation with the LSA.
- Expectations are kept high for all students.
- Independent working is encouraged, with the LSA making sure she doesn't give more help than is really needed.
- Group work is used as a means of fostering cooperation, collaboration and the development of social skills.

In the third model, support is focused on the individual child who may spend part of the day working on a one-to-one basis with their support worker on individually designed tasks. Where they are working with the whole class or in a group, they have their support worker by their side helping, prompting and encouraging. The support worker has often worked with the child for some time and knows them well. They may have developed a particular expertise and feel confident in giving the child the best possible chance to succeed in the mainstream.

This approach can work well (Alliance for Inclusive Education (AIE) 2001) where:

- individual pupils have high-level support needs
- it is essential for the LSA to be additionally trained or to possess particular skills
- the pupil finds it difficult to communicate with strangers
- support requires a high level of intimacy and sensitivity
- the LSA is aware of the danger of overprotection and allows the child to take risks
- the LSA respects the child's views and opinions and will act as an advocate for them
- the LSA doesn't act as a barrier between the child and the class teacher or between the child and their friends.

In even the smallest primary school, the job of appointing and managing LSAs is a key one if an inclusive ethos is to be promoted. In their recent guidance for schools (DfEE 2001a), the DfEE stress the importance of:

- defining responsibilities clearly
- providing clear deployment within a flexible framework
- creating partnerships with other people involved in education
- creating partnership among teaching assistants
- reviewing performance and promoting development.

Each LSA should have a clear job description (Lorenz 1999b) which is reviewed at least once a year. When newly appointed, they should be given an induction pack containing information about the school and ideally be allowed to shadow another LSA for a short while to get the hang of the job. They need to be given time within their working day to liaise and plan with the teacher or teachers they are supporting. They should also have regular opportunities to talk informally with their line manager about their job and to share any concerns they may have about what they are being asked to do.

This must be handled delicately, as few LSAs will feel sufficiently confident to criticise a teacher directly. However, they are often the first people to notice when a child is unhappy or is failing to cope with the work they are being asked to do. Where the partnership between teacher and LSA is not going well, there needs to be someone sufficiently senior to build bridges or explain tactfully to either party what they might do to resolve the problem.

Chapter 5

First Steps for Secondary Schools

Creating a positive school ethos

There is no doubt, as Thomas (1999) comments, that inclusion will be the single most important educational issue for at least the first half of the 21st century. National governments across the globe will, in the decades ahead, be seeking to make schools more inclusive. However, this presents some serious challenges for teachers, because schools in the 20th century have been almost exclusively segregative. Comprehensive education for all has never, in reality, meant all. Instead, curricula and pastoral systems in mainstream schools have developed as if 2 per cent of the population did not exist.

By the time that the grammar schools and secondary moderns were being amalgamated to form the new comprehensives, the place of the special school in the system was already firmly established and not even the most far-sighted educational administrator considered including these pupils in their new schools. Special educators, as Thomas and Loxley (2001) note, by devising ever-more elaborate forms of assessment and teaching had already convinced the teaching profession that 'special children' could only thrive under their specialised regimes and that 'special skills' were required to teach them. Despite a lack of hard evidence to support this position, the belief in special schools as a good thing has continued alongside the current debate on inclusion.

Most secondary teachers have had little experience of pupils with significant learning, communication or physical needs and even fewer have worked with them in the ordinary classroom. Few have thought about the realities of inclusion or questioned commonly held beliefs about children with significant disabilities (see Figure 5.1). As the manager of a secondary school aiming to become more inclusive, you will need to ask staff to review their attitudes, to take on board the fundamental belief that comprehensive education really is for everyone and to accept that inclusion is, essentially, just a matter of extending the comprehensive ideal one stage further. This chapter will hopefully help you to identify some of the key issues and start you out on what might be a very long road.

EVERYONE KNOWS THAT
Pupils with significant disabilities:

Fall outside the range of differences that can be accommodated in an ordinary school.

Learn very little even with special teaching and learn nothing from ordinary teaching approaches.

Require constant adult attention and thus must be in very small classes.

Drain the teacher's energy and discourage and depress all but the most special kind of person.

Demand so much teacher attention that they detract from the learning of more able peers.

Need highly specialised teaching and therapeutic procedures which are beyond the ordinary teacher's ability to learn without additional training.

Will be rejected, ridiculed and exploited by non-disabled students in the mainstream.

Will suffer damage to their self-esteem as a consequence of constant rejection and the failure to measure up.

Are better off with 'their own kind' where they can get the special help they need.

Figure 5.1 (after O'Brien and Forest 1998)

In looking at your school as it is now, you are likely to be faced by:

- pressure from governors, parents, the LEA and the government to raise standards, particularly the number of students gaining grades A–C at GCSE level
- staff shortages and real difficulty in finding suitable supply cover to release staff for training or development work
- yet more new initiatives to implement and a staff suffering from innovation overload
- pressure from the Department for Education and Skills (DfES) to increase setting and streaming as the best way to raise standards

- financial incentives from central government to encourage you to become a specialist school with a more selective intake
- a building largely unsuited to the needs of pupils with mobility problems, with narrow doorways, long corridors and specialist rooms reached via flights of stairs
- rooms with poor acoustic qualities or inadequate lighting, making the effective use of hearing or low vision aids particularly difficult.

Nevertheless, despite these real difficulties, increasing numbers of secondary schools are developing a more inclusive philosophy and there is no reason why you could not be among that number. Tools such as the *Index for Inclusion* (Booth *et al*. 2000) now exist to help in the process of inclusive school development. However, it is important that it remains a collaborative process involving staff, students, parents, governors and members of the local community. Unfortunately, as Fullan (1991) points out, implementation of those changes that positively affect the learning of students is difficult to achieve as it involves teachers:

- acquiring new knowledge
- adopting new teaching styles and
- modifying their beliefs and values.

As Hopkins comments (1997), altering your ways of thinking and doing can be painful so it is essential that schools ensure that individuals are supported throughout this inevitable but difficult and challenging process. School implementation works best when a clear and practical focus for development is linked to simultaneous work on the internal conditions within the school. The commitment of all those involved has to be maintained throughout any implementation phase – this is at least as important a role for school managers as any concept of visionary leadership.

Nevertheless you do need to provide clear leadership and to provide the vision of where the school is heading. Experience has shown that inclusive schools welcome diversity and foster the development of friendships alongside the achievement of learning goals for all their students. In the inclusive school:

- classroom climate is considered alongside the curriculum
- the environment is warm, positive and accepting
- all students are valued as individuals
- students learn respect and tolerance for one another
- students learn ways of working together so everyone can participate.

To work towards becoming more inclusive, your SMT needs to set aside time:

- to plan together to meet the needs of all students
- to consider the social effects of pupil groupings
- to look at the way support is used throughout the school
- to consider the place of disability awareness in the school curriculum

- to review the use of peer support and the ways in which students can be involved in developing their own learning programmes
- to consider alternative forms of accreditation at Key Stage 4
- to look at the use of homework across the school.

Every teacher in an inclusive school:

- accepts responsibility for the learning of all the students in the classes they teach
- gets to know their students before modifying the curriculum or the classroom environment
- works towards full participation of all students
- models positive social interactions with all students
- involves the peer group in meeting the needs of all students
- celebrates the achievement of all students.

Remember above all else that friendships with peers are often the key to a young person's sense of identity and emotional security. To foster the development of friendships:

- provide ample opportunities for students to interact naturally without close support
- encourage the use of peer tutoring and 'buddy' systems
- use circle time to explore feelings and establish 'circles of friends' to support individuals
- make sure your anti-bullying policy provides emotional security for all students.

Collaboration and partnership

> For many teachers the thought of having a student with a disability in their class seems like a completely unrealistic position if not a terrifying nightmare. Yet these same teachers are often unaware of the possible minor adaptations which could be made in the classroom to accommodate each student (Kunc 1984).

Do you have teachers in your school who feel threatened and deskilled by the move towards inclusion? If so then it is important that:

- they are encouraged to verbalise genuine concerns
- they are given opportunities to share their worries with supportive colleagues
- they are encouraged to work in collaborative problem-solving teams.

Teachers need time not only to develop their teaching skills but also to consider the implications of the changes in practice required. As Ainscow (1995) observes, schools that value enquiry and reflection find it easier to sustain momentum and to monitor the extent of actual change. For the success of inclusion depends on the motivation of those directly involved in its implementation at classroom level and their ability to devise changes to the system through reflection and practice (Wolger 1998). Working in teams allows teachers to improve their teaching skills by learning from each other. It also allows human and material resources to be shared or combined in order that they can be used to best effect. By sharing responsibility for pupils with unique learning needs, staff can begin to overcome the isolation felt by many teachers in self-contained classrooms.

Within the secondary school, there are many opportunities for staff to develop teamworking (see Figure 5.2).

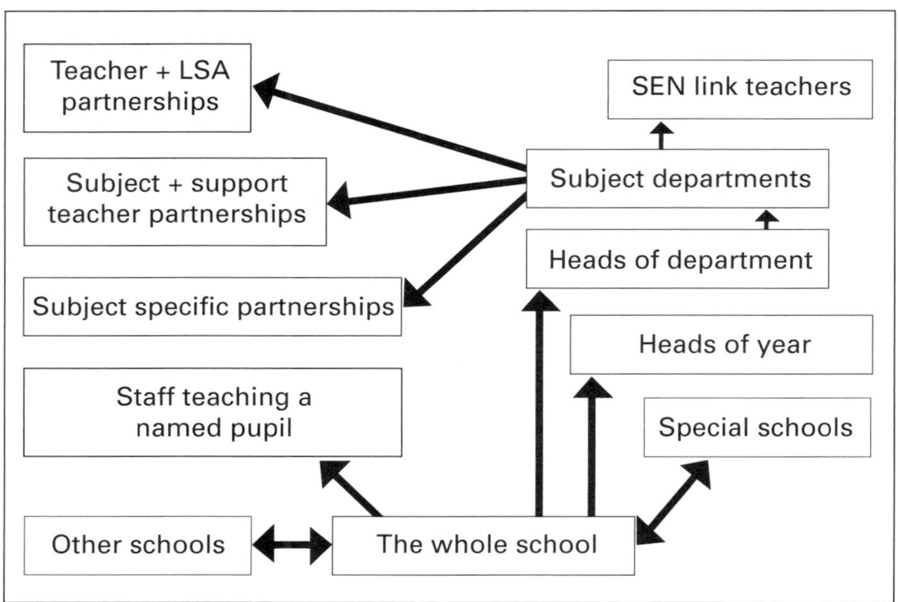

Figure 5.2 Opportunities for teamwork

To work together effectively as team players, as Reif and Heimburge (1996) point out, staff need:

- a supportive and open sharing environment where ideas and teaching styles are respected and appreciated
- colleagues who have the ability to listen carefully to each other's needs and wants and who can offer constructive criticism and praise
- common goals for students and teachers
- a common vision for students
- reasonable standards and expectations of students and team members.

Team development needs to be ongoing with regular opportunities for team members to meet and discuss progress. At the whole-school level, teamwork is important to ensure that all staff contribute to a shared vision. There should be agreement as to the purpose of inclusive education and the relative priority to be given to academic goals as opposed to the development of social skills, independence and participation. All staff must understand the role of teaching assistants and support teachers and the part the subject teacher is expected to play in the design, delivery and evaluation of teaching programmes for disabled students. A termly staff meeting chaired by the SENCO or part of a staff development day can usefully be devoted to these issues. Wherever possible, support staff should also be included as their insights into special needs issues can often be extremely helpful in developing the understanding of subject teachers.

Heads of department, meeting regularly, are in an excellent position to work collaboratively to ensure that there is an agreed policy regarding:

- setting and streaming
- team teaching
- the use of LSAs
- assessment and record-keeping
- alternative accreditation.

Similarly, heads of year can adopt common practices with regard to:

- bullying
- disability awareness
- mentoring, buddy systems and circles of friends
- access to extra-curricular activities for disabled students.

At the faculty or departmental level, teamworking can be particularly effective, especially if it leads to collaborative teaching. Whitmore High School in Harrow described by Sebba and Sachdev (1997), for example, uses departmental meetings to focus primarily on curriculum development with the aim of enabling individual staff to develop an appropriate learning environment for all students. Their aim is essentially a preventative one. However, there are also opportunities within departmental meetings for difficulties with individual students to be addressed and solutions found collaboratively, without the attribution of blame.

Where a school has only a small number of students with exceptional needs, one very effective approach is for all staff who work with that student to meet together on a termly or half-termly basis to discuss concerns and resolve difficulties. In some instances an outside professional can be brought in to facilitate the discussion, although this is often counterproductive, inhibiting staff from offering their own solutions. On the other hand, the presence of a parent can be very helpful. Even when there are no particular problems, such meetings can be important in:

- helping staff gain a shared understanding of the student across settings
- highlighting strengths not otherwise recognised
- identifying supportive peers
- reaching agreement on appropriate academic and social goals.

Traditionally, the secondary school teacher has been the only adult in the classroom. However, in the inclusive school, the norm is for there to be at least two adults involved in curriculum delivery. The second adult may be another subject teacher, an SEN or support teacher from within the school or from an LEA support service, or an LSA. If the partnership works well, teaming will make their teaching more effective and will improve the individual growth and development of all the students in the class.

Being involved in a team is said to change teachers by:

- generating a new understanding of their own teaching style
- bringing forth a renewed sense of enthusiasm
- providing a healthier more balanced environment for everyone involved
- inspiring them to stay abreast of current developments
- giving them the opportunity to extend their interpersonal skills.

Some of the many approaches to teamworking, including collaborative classroom consultation, peer coaching and partnership teaching, are described in my earlier book *Effective In-Class Support* (Lorenz 1998b). In this book, I stress the need for staff working in partnership to meet on a regular basis to share curricular information and provide feedback on individual students. This can be particularly difficult in a secondary school where support teachers and assistants may be working with a large number of different teachers across the week and are expected to use breaks and lunch-times for other duties. Nevertheless, problems can be alleviated once subject teachers are aware of the difficulties support staff face and have spent time thinking about the role of the supporter.

Effective schools will set aside staff development time for teachers and support staff to work together and look at ways each can help the other to do their job more effectively. They will also seek out partners in the locality, be they other mainstream schools or special schools, with whom they can share ideas and swap expertise. The government in its Programme for Action (DfEE 1998a) talks about special schools developing practical links with mainstream schools and working with their mainstream colleagues to plan support for individual students. Similarly mainstream partnerships and support networks can provide additional support and encouragement when the journey towards inclusion starts getting tough.

If this approach is to work for you, it is important that you discover the nature and extent of specialist knowledge and expertise of staff in your local schools and its relevance to your student population. You then need to discuss the most effective ways that knowledge and expertise can be shared to the mutual benefit of staff and students in both participating schools. Never underestimate the skills of your own staff or the contribution they could make to the development of other schools.

Ensuring curriculum access

Traditional definitions of the curriculum (Armstrong 1998) reflect the view that it is concerned purely with specifying and producing particular targets, performances and behaviours in students which are explicit and testable according to certain narrowly defined criteria. In contrast is the view that curriculum is not simply about content, but about:

- how the subject matter is to be organised
- the way in which it is to be delivered
- the educational purposes it serves
- the learning outcomes it is intended to achieve and
- the methods by which such outcomes are measured.

The way schools are organised, what they teach and how it is taught are expressions of their values and ethos as well as those of the wider society. According to Zemelman (1998) the inclusive school is one where there is:

- more choice for students
- more cooperative, collaborative activity
- more in-class support and less withdrawal
- more experimental, inductive, hands-on learning
- more responsibility transferred to students for their work
- more mixed ability classrooms, less setting and streaming
- more active learning with students doing, talking and collaborating
- more varied and cooperative roles for teachers, supporters and parents
- more emphasis on learning the key concepts and principles of a subject
- more attention to the emotional needs and varying learning styles of students
- more reliance on teachers' descriptions of student progress, less on standardised tests.

If pupils are to be offered an effective learning environment, it is essential that your school building and the teaching areas within it are fit for use. If you are catering for students with limited mobility, look at where specialist rooms are sited and at how rooms are laid out. Ask a wheelchair user to carry out an audit of the building including access to rooms, practical equipment, ease of movement around the school, use of toilets and dining halls. Alternatively, borrow a wheelchair and do the survey yourself. You will soon realise the problems disabled students face.

Many helpful adaptations, e.g. painting handrails white for students with visual impairments, are easy to make and cost little more than time and commitment. Others will require more effort, but could easily form the basis for a GCSE Technology Project. All schools are expected to incorporate access issues into their School Development Plan and all can now apply for funding via the Schools Access Initiative. This funding can be used not only to increase physical access but also for developments to aid curricular access, so the brief is very wide.

To learn effectively students need to be in an environment where there are:

- high expectations
- good role models and
- opportunities for collaboration.

If students with physical, sensory or learning difficulties are placed with disaffected and poorly motivated peers in bottom sets or special needs groupings within the classroom, these may be denied. It is therefore always worth considering whether subjects could be taught in mixed ability groups or whether individual students could be placed with more able peers.

Sally is a young lady with Down's Syndrome who attends her local high school. The school sets for all subjects and Sally, as a slow learner, spends most of her time in bottom sets. A quiet well-mannered girl when she first came to the school, Sally now swears like a trooper and spends much of her time messing about in lessons, as do her peers.

Danny on the other hand, while also having severe learning difficulties, was placed from the start in the fourth of five sets, where most students are prepared to settle down to work. As his LSA remarks 'Since we have to differentiate all his work individually, it really doesn't matter about the ability level of the class. However, the other students collaborate well with Danny and set him a good example.'

Another important factor to bear in mind in ensuring curriculum access for all students is that of individual learning style. This must form a key part of any differentiated learning programme. As England (2001) comments 'Instructional activities and products may be differentiated in terms of student interests, student skill level, and student learning styles. Differentiated instruction is not so much the "what" but the "how" the students will learn.' Ron Babbage and his colleagues (Babbage *et al.* 2001) stress the importance of understanding individual learning styles. Some students like to become quickly engaged in practical activities; others prefer to reflect on their options before becoming involved. Some pupils demand high levels of adult support and guidance; others prefer to work things out for themselves or in collaboration with peers.

In response to a variety of preferred learning styles, teachers in the inclusive classroom need to offer a range of teaching approaches and respond flexibly to individual needs. As Peterson and Tamor (2001) remark, the traditional approach of grouping pupils crudely by ability and then teaching to the middle is doomed to failure. In direct contrast, they advocate multi-level teaching whereby students of differing abilities and different learning styles can each be challenged and obtain the support they need to learn effectively in mixed ability groups and classes. In the secondary school, where teachers may see individual students only once or twice a week, it may be difficult to develop an adequate knowledge of individual learners to teach them effectively. Schools therefore need to reflect upon their culture and develop the processes required to gain knowledge of each pupil's learning profile.

It is also important for teachers to be open-minded as to the objectives of any lesson for an individual learner. While ideally it should be possible to differentiate the content of any subject area to make it appropriate for learners at any level, the preparation and planning required to give them full access has not always been done. Nevertheless, learning opportunities can be designed to focus not on the acquisition of new subject specific knowledge, but on a range of other equally relevant outcomes such as:

- problem-solving
- making choices
- peer interaction
- collaboration
- communication
- memory building
- independence.

Where teachers have got together with colleagues and spent time analysing the content of the National Curriculum in their particular subject area, it has been possible to provide Curriculum Maps (Hutchinson 2001) which enable any subject to be taught to students working towards Level 1 at the same time as to others working at Level 5 or anywhere in-between (see Table 5.1).

These maps will determine the conceptual level of the work set and can then be combined with knowledge about the student's level of language understanding, the teaching approach which best suits their learning style and the level of additional support required by each learner, to produce a detailed teaching strategy. Clearly this is not something that can be left to an unqualified LSA, but must be integral to the teacher's overall planning which is then shared with support staff.

CURRICULUM MAP CHRONOLOGICAL UNDERSTANDING IN HISTORY
Teaching objective: Place events, people and changes in correct periods of time.
LEVEL w1 Identify difference between pictures of young people now and as babies. Distinguish between old and new objects. Sequence events experienced by student. Sequence the school day into a simple order.
LEVEL 1 Sequence pictures of young person at different ages, then relatives and other familiar adults. Sequence pictures of related objects belonging to people of different ages. Sequence objects, pictures and events in student's life to produce chronology. Sequence the days of the week and use as a very simple timeline.
LEVEL 2 Sequence events and objects studied within a historical context. Place a selection of pictures/toys/artefacts in chronological order and answer questions about the oldest and the newest. Sequence the months of the year and use as a timeline, e.g. as a calendar of the school year. Use timelines with non-standard units to sequence items such as several generations of family photographs.
LEVEL 3 Use timelines marked in decades to sequence objects/people/events beyond living memory. Use timelines marked in centuries to sequence and compare events/objects/people in historical time. Develop an understanding of the division of historical time into periods where people/objects/events can be located.
LEVEL 4 Develop an understanding of the use of dates to locate people and events in time. Begin to make appropriate uses of dates and chronological terms in structured work.
LEVEL 5 Make appropriate uses of dates and chronological terms to produce structured work.

Table 5.1 Example of a Curriculum Map

Alternatives to exclusion

The term EBD (educational and behavioural difficulty) is one that is widely and unquestioningly used throughout the UK (Thomas and Loxley 2001). Despite the abolition of categories of SEN following the Warnock Report of 1978 and the Education Act 1981 which followed it, children continue to be categorised, statements issued and resources allocated on the basis of children's EBDs. In earlier times, there was a clear distinction in the minds of teachers between the disturbed and the disturbing – the first were in need of treatment and the second of punishment. In recent years, however, the whole population of children who fail to fit neatly into our increasingly centralised education system is deemed to have SEN.

Despite an increasing emphasis (Elton 1989) on the need for educationalists to give at least as much emphasis to school-focused issues as to the analysis and treatment of children's behaviour, there is little sign of this happening in many schools. Exclusion rates continue to rise (Parsons 1999) and there is a steady growth in the number and size of segregated EBD schools, pupil referral units and within-school 'sin bins' or support units. The belief that children who behave badly are deviant or disturbed is clearly more comfortable for many teachers than the idea that it is they or their schools that are causing or aggravating the problem. It is also more acceptable to consider the child as having 'special needs' that should be addressed, preferably by somebody else, than to admit that it is the needs of the school and of the other pupils that are at the heart of the matter.

This clinical approach is often unhelpful in restoring calm and order to our schools. Instead a different view about how to respond to difficult behaviour in school can emerge out of current thinking on inclusion. The inclusive school should best be seen as a humane environment rather than a set of pre-existing structures and systems for dealing with misbehaviour. As we all know, schools are riddled with rules and practices which are rarely reviewed and are often pointless or outmoded. Yet pupils who flaunt these rules or question their validity are frequently considered deviant. Teachers regularly shout at pupils or behave unreasonably, yet their behaviour is condoned. Similar behaviours on the part of students will almost certainly lead to sanctions.

Couple this reality with the development of secondary curricula which seem increasingly meaningless to non-academic pupils and it is not surprising that more and more students are becoming disaffected. For some, the best solution is truancy or early pregnancy. For others, more fun and peer group status can be afforded by challenging the system from within. So how useful is the concept of EBD or is it merely a smokescreen behind which schools can hide to avoid addressing the real issues?

Despite the move towards more inclusion, a recent survey (Croll and Moses 2000) found two-thirds of primary head teachers considered that more children with EBD should be in special schools. Further, only 2 per cent of teachers attributed behavioural difficulties to schools and teachers. The attitude of those in secondary schools is, almost undoubtedly, even more pronounced, if the comparative rates of exclusion in the two sectors are taken into account. While we cannot condone violence or deny that a small proportion of children do experience significant emotional difficulties, we know that the rates of aberrant behaviour found in schools vary widely from institution to institution and have more to do with school ethos than with indices of deprivation or disadvantage. So what is it that makes a difference?

Certainly there is little evidence that bureaucratic responses, such as writing an anti-bullying policy, are effective on their own unless there has been active involvement by the whole school community. As Skrtic (1991) notes, they can comprise an assortment of symbols and ceremonies which look and sound like sensible action, but do little to change the school culture. Thomas and Loxley (2001) suggest that while most schools have moved from a merely therapeutic response to inappropriate behaviour to a whole-school approach, what is now required is to move on again towards creating a humane environment (see Figure 5.3).

THERAPEUTIC →	WHOLE SCHOOL →	HUMANE ENVIRONMENT
* Counselling. * Behaviour modification. * Group work. * Drugs e.g. Ritalin. * Family therapy.	* Updating bullying policy. * Ensuring better liaison with school psychologist. * Rationalising report card system. * Establishing clearer guidelines for moving between stages of SEN Code of Practice. * Setting up governor link with learning support department. * Improving IEPs.	* Having more carpeted areas in school. * Ensuring litter is cleared regularly. * Ensuring a plentiful supply of regularly maintained drinking fountains. * Taking steps to discipline teachers who bully students. * Staggering playtimes, school start and finish times in large schools to reduce congestion. * Ensuring fair queuing systems at lunchtime. * Establishing a School Council whose views are routinely considered by governing body. * Reducing number of whole-school assemblies. * Ensuring toilets are regularly cleaned. * Allowing students to stay in at break and lunchtimes. * Providing lockable lockers for all students.

Figure 5.3 Creating a humane environment (adapted from Thomas and Loxley 2001)

The ethos of the school is critical in creating either a culture in which exclusion is relatively frequent and seen as a necessary sanction, or one in which exclusion is viewed as a sign of failure. In their study of Scottish schools, Munn *et al.* (2000) found that low-excluding schools had head teachers who believed it was the job of the school to educate all pupils, not just the well motivated and well behaved. They saw it as a collective responsibility of all staff to motivate pupils, to make learning fun and to make all pupils feel valued. In such schools, an inclusive ethos was seen to be not just about supporting pupils and providing them with an enjoyable learning experience, but also about providing real practical support for staff when problems occurred.

A key part of a school's ethos concerns curriculum provision and organisation. It is already well known (Sukhnandan and Lee 1998) that grouping pupils by ability leads to those in bottom groups feeling less valued and, as a consequence, encourages them to adopt disruptive behaviours as a way of disguising their academic failure. As Postman (1996) comments 'There is no question that listlessness, ennui and even violence in school are related to the fact that students have no useful role to play in society'.

The recent moves away from an overly prescriptive and academic curriculum for 14–16-year-old pupils offering them the option of:

- vocational GCSE courses
- alternative accreditation at Key Stage 4
- extended work experience
- college-based courses and
- youth and community projects

is undoubtedly a step in the right direction but is far from commonplace. As Cullen *et al.* (2001) have found, when carefully set up, well-run, monitored and evaluated, alternative approaches have been effective in preventing exclusions and creating more positive routes for young people. Nevertheless, it will be some time before these options are on offer in the majority of schools.

However flexible the curriculum in Key Stage 4, it is important that schools realise that the seeds of disaffection are sown much earlier. Low-excluding schools in the Scottish study were typically characterised by extensive after-school and lunchtime activities. Pupils' efforts on the sports field, in music, art and drama was considered as of equal value to academic prowess. Personal and social education were high on their list of important curriculum areas and ways were found in which all students could contribute positively to the life of the school from Year 7 onwards. This is particularly important for students with learning or physical difficulties who are just as likely to display inappropriate behaviours as their so-called EBD peers.

At the same time as valuing pupils, schools need to have high expectation of student behaviour and means by which acceptable behaviour can be recognised and rewarded. Secondary teachers in the UK are notoriously sparing in their use of praise. Yet any effective behavioural strategy involves a praise/criticism ratio of at least 3:1. The idea of 'catching pupils getting it right' is crucial in the inclusive school. On the other hand, the overuse of praise, as Smith (1998) notes, may limit the opportunity for students to develop their own decision-making abilities and can reduce their ability to self-evaluate.

Chapter 6

First Steps for SENCOs

Developing the SENCO role

There is no doubt that the role of the SENCO is not what it was. Not only are mainstream schools taking in an increasingly diverse population of children, but they are being expected to change their organisation, their ethos and their teaching approaches to reflect a more inclusive philosophy. As key players in this process of change, SENCOs are increasingly being expected to 'manoeuvre their schools into positions of maximum receptiveness to the challenges that lie ahead' (Shuttleworth 2000). If you find yourself in just such a position, or are considering expanding your existing role and becoming more proactive in the change process, this chapter is for you. In it are some of the central issues that need to be addressed along the road to inclusion and some insights are offered into what might be effective in your school.

The nub of the SENCO's role is, in collaboration with others, to help determine the strategic development of the SEN policy and provision in the school, thus breaking down barriers to learning and participation.

Duties listed in the revised Code of Practice (DfES 2001) include:

- overseeing the day-to-day operation of the school's SEN policy
- coordinating provision for children with SEN
- liaising with and advising fellow teachers
- managing LSAs
- overseeing the records of all children with SEN
- liaising with parents of children with SEN
- contributing to the in-service training of staff
- liaising with external agencies.

To do all this effectively, while maintaining your sanity, you will require a wide range of skills (see Figure 6.1).

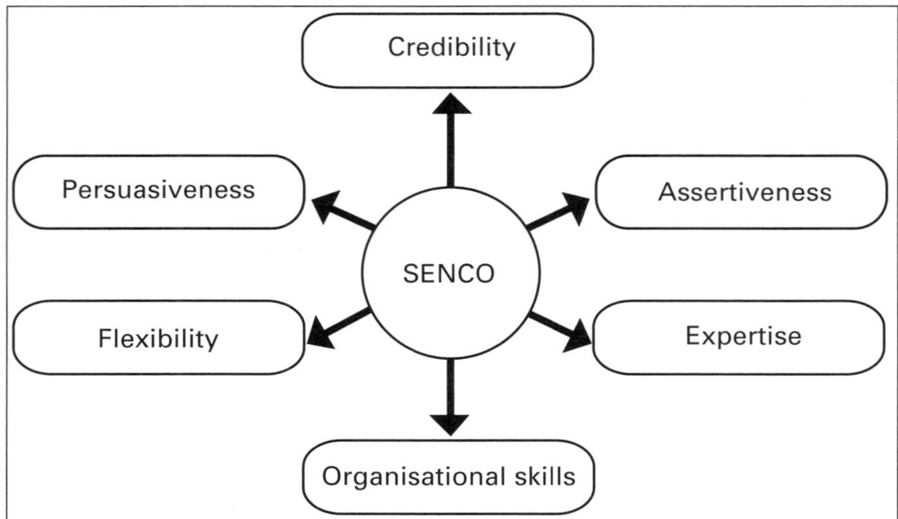

Figure 6.1 The effective SENCO (after Shuttleworth 2000)

Many SENCOs started out their careers as glorified remedial teachers, who spent most of their time protecting vulnerable children from inappropriate teaching approaches in mainstream classes and relieving colleagues of the need to differentiate or address individual needs. However, as the wisdom on children with special needs has changed, young people are being withdrawn less from mainstream lessons to be taught by specialists in special settings. Instead, class and subject teachers are taking on ever greater responsibility for teaching these pupils in ordinary classes. As a direct consequence, SENCOs are spending progressively less time teaching pupils with SEN and more time advising colleagues.

If you are to do this effectively, as Shuttleworth (2000) stresses, it is essential that you maintain credibility with your colleagues by modelling good practice in any classes you teach. Make sure your teaching demonstrates:

- effective classroom organisation
- differentiated methods and resources
- clear teaching objectives linked to IEPs
- joint planning with support staff
- high expectations of all pupils
- constant use of praise and encouragement
- inclusion of all pupils in class activities.

Only then can you work productively with other staff to 'create and foster commitment and confidence among staff to meeting the needs of pupils with SEN' (*ibid*).

Whenever possible, try to team teach with colleagues to provide support and model alternative ways of working. Find regular opportunities to discuss effective teaching strategies. Consult and share, but never be seen to know best. Remember that the most effective way to ensure change in an organisation is to involve as many people as possible in policy development. Colleagues need to feel a sense of ownership. Look at your current SEN policy and check with colleagues on its user friendliness. Are tasks clearly defined and unambiguous? Is policy reflected in practice and if not why not? Are there ways in which you can help colleagues be more effective in creating inclusive classrooms? If you feel your policy is failing to provide a suitable framework for the development of inclusive practice, think about initiating a whole-school policy review.

Schools, as they become more inclusive, will move away from the view that it is pupils with special needs who are failing within the educational system towards the belief that it is the pupils who are being failed by the system itself. The onus is therefore on schools to change, rather than attempt to prop up individual pupils. As SENCO, you have a key role in helping class and subject teachers to adapt and modify the taught curriculum to meet the needs of all learners, however challenging this may be in some cases. You also have a role in helping senior managers understand how policies and practices need to change to reflect a more inclusive philosophy.

Before setting out to effect change, Shuttleworth (2000) suggests you apply the TWIRL test to your school to assess where you are in respect of:

TRAINING for all staff on SEN issues.
WHOLE SCHOOL responses to inclusion.
INVOLVEMENT of the Head in monitoring the SEN policy.
RESOURCE allocation for SEN.
LOCATION of any SEN facility or base. (See Figure 6.2.)

Training in SEN for all staff.	**W**hole school response to inclusion.	**I**nvolvement of Head in monitoring SEN policy.	**R**esource allocation for SEN.	**L**ocation of SEN facility.
Compulsory SEN training for all staff.	Use of *Index for Inclusion* by whole school.	Head actively involved in monitoring pupil progress.	SENCO responsible for managing adequate budget.	Resource base centrally sited and used by all pupils and staff.
School-funded training available for all staff.	Inclusion working group in place.	Regular meetings between Head and SENCO.	SEN budget under control of SMT but most bids accepted.	No distinct SEN base. Resources spread throughout school.
Training available for teachers only.	Some discussion at staff and curriculum meetings.	Head kept informed via SENCO briefing papers.	SEN budget allocated to class teachers or faculties.	Resource base at end of corridor and used only by SEN pupils.
Little training available.	Inclusion rarely discussed by staff.	Little interest in SEN shown by Head.	No identified resources for SEN.	SEN withdrawal unit in isolated hut across playground.

Figure 6.2 Applying the TWIRL test

This should give you an appropriate focus for discussions with your head teacher, governors or SMT. At the same time, it is useful to carry out an audit of need to determine whether there are:

- individual pupils whose needs are currently not being met
- particular faculties or curriculum areas where staff need help with differentiation or in developing more positive attitudes towards pupils with SEN
- individual teachers or LSAs who need personal support in curriculum delivery, behaviour management or teamwork.

Improving communication across the school

The revised Code of Practice (DfES 2001) creates the expectation that SENCOs will liaise extensively with their teacher colleagues, with external agencies and with parents. Such liaison, however, is time-consuming and the problems may be equally great in large schools – where many teachers, professionals and parents need to be kept informed – as in small schools where the SENCO is likely to have less time and fewer facilities. The key relationship for any SENCO is that with the head teacher. As the Teacher Training Agency notes (TTA 1998), effective coordination of SEN results in head teachers and other senior managers who 'recognise that the curriculum must be relevant to all pupils, by taking SEN into account in the formulation and implementation of policies throughout the school'.

To increase the ability of the SENCO to influence school development planning, the National Association for Special Educational Needs (NASEN 2000) recommends that he or she is a full member of the SMT. In smaller schools, where this is not practicable, they should hold a position at least equivalent to that of the literacy or numeracy coordinator. While there are still a few schools where the head teacher also holds the post of SENCO, this is considered undesirable except as a last resort as it prevents the SENCO from acting as a link between the key players within the school, at the centre of a series of effective partnerships (see Figure 6.3).

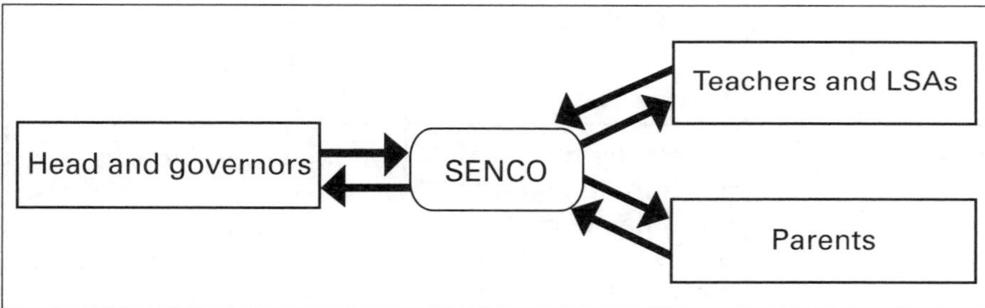

Figure 6.3 The SENCO role

In working with your head teacher it is important that you establish a regular pattern of meetings and use these, ideally, to:

- celebrate the achievement of pupils with special needs
- share views in an open and honest manner
- develop mutual respect and confidence
- establish the extent of your authority for decision-making
- provide feedback on the implementation of the SEN policy
- agree areas for development.

Time is always a problem. Nevertheless, it might be worth your while to consider providing termly reports for the head teacher on progress to date and key issues to be addressed, using a proforma such as that shown in Table 6.1. These feedback sheets can then be used as an agenda for discussion and form the basis of your annual report for governors.

SEN PROGRESS REVIEW
Welcome Junior School – Autumn Term

KEY AREA	SUCCESSES TO DATE	AREAS FOR DEVELOPMENT
CURRICULUM	Statemented students participating well in Literacy Hour. Support now being used to facilitate participation instead of 1:1 work.	Differentiation of science materials still relatively poor. Could consider: a) links with special school b) staff working group c) protected time for development.
BEHAVIOUR	Buddy system working well in helping Yr 3 pupils settle in. Could usefully be developed in other year groups.	Boisterous behaviour of some pupils in playground denying others their right to play in safety. Need to involve pupils in finding equitable solution.
STAFF TRAINING	All LSAs successfully completed LEA induction course. Staff feeling more confident in their skills and more aware of need for teamworking.	Training for teaching staff on effective use of support staff now required. Could consider: a) using next training day b) buying in outside trainer c) producing staff handbook.
RESOURCES	Rearrangement of furniture in dining room has permitted pupils with mobility problems to collect own lunch.	Ongoing problems in accessing art room on first floor. Consider: a) bid for access funds b) resiting art and craft resources.
	Allocation of 2hrs secretarial support for SENCO of real benefit.	Still no private room for meeting parents or counselling pupils. Consider designating music room for SENCO use twice a week.

Table 6.1 Example of a proforma

As an overworked SENCO who is being pulled in all directions, you will almost certainly find that effective liaison with colleagues can be a particular nightmare, especially in a large school or where you are managing a team of LSAs. Try to avoid being accosted in corridors. Instead, set up regular surgery times when you can meet with staff in rotation, by appointment or on a drop-in basis. Make sure that you are protected from other duties during these sessions, take the phone off the hook and arrange to have student files and other relevant resources to hand.

Use communication systems already in place in your school to pass on SEN information. A recent working party on the role of the SENCO (DfEE 1998b) identified a diversity of systems that could be used to communicate information:

- morning staff briefings
- after-school staff meetings
- departmental meetings
- staffroom noticeboards
- staff pigeon holes
- staff newsletters
- lesson planning sheets
- pupil record sheets
- annual reports to parents.

These can then be supplemented, where necessary, by:

- a weekly SEN briefing note or termly SEN newsletter
- individual child profiles highlighting key statement targets
- summary sheets for annual reviews or case conferences
- information slips in the staffroom used by staff to pass on observations or ask for help.

In the secondary sector, departmental or faculty link teachers can be useful in aiding communication. However, it is important that they are of sufficient status to influence colleagues and that they do not act as a barrier between the SENCO and subject teachers. A link teacher need not be an expert in SEN or teach more pupils with special needs than their colleagues, but they should:

- communicate information to colleagues from the SENCO
- feedback information on individual pupils
- encourage colleagues in the development of differentiated resources
- ensure SEN issues are on the agenda of all departmental meetings
- support colleagues in the formulation and implementation of IEPs.

With the implementation of the SEN and Disability Act 2001, SENCOs will have an increasingly important role to play in ensuring that all staff are fully aware of its implications and the need for strategic planning. The Act places a duty on schools 'to ensure that disabled pupils are not placed at a substantial disadvantage, in comparison to pupils who are not disabled, in relation to education and associated services', i.e.

- accessibility of the building
- participation in the curriculum
- timetabling and pupil grouping
- assessment and examination arrangements
- involvement in after-school clubs and trips out.

Even though the full force of the legislation will not be felt until September 2002 at the earliest, you and your colleagues should already be thinking carefully about the changes you will need to make to curriculum delivery and school practices. This is an excellent time to look at existing working groups and teams to make sure that the new legislation is on their agenda.

Using support effectively

As Thomas and his colleagues (Thomas *et al.* 1998) note, the effective delivery of support is crucial for successful inclusion, yet surprisingly little attention has been paid to the ways support works in classrooms. The *National Standards for Special Educational Needs Coordinators* (TTA 1998), cites 'the efficient and effective deployment of staff and resources' as a key requirement of the SENCO role and, therefore, it is up to you to ensure that this is one area that is not neglected.

Look at your existing set-up and be clear about who is available to offer support.

- How many hours of LSA time do you have across the school?
- Are these hours flexible or determined by the LEA or by their other commitments?
- What particular skills do they possess and how do they prefer to work?
- How many hours of additional teacher time are available for in-class or small-group support?
- Are these teachers SEN or subject specialists?
- How much time can you devote to supporting colleagues yourself?
- Do you have parent helpers you can rely on to provide additional help in class, in the playground or on school trips?

Carry out an annual audit of pupils' support needs, specifying the type and amount of support to best promote their inclusion.

- Identify those pupils who need a personal assistant most of the time.
- Specify the particular tasks that need to be performed and any specialist skills required by the supporter, e.g. Braille, British Sign Language, lifting and handling.
- Identify pupils who need access to a support teacher or teaching assistant but are able to share support or work with different supporters.
- Determine the curriculum areas in which support is required.
- For each lesson, decide whether support is best provided by a teaching assistant, an SEN support teacher or a subject specialist.
- Arrange student support needs in priority order to ensure resources are used to best effect (DfEE 1998b).
- Set up a support timetable which attempts to match staff skills and availability with student needs.

- Make sure cover arrangements are in place if staff are ill or on training.
- Where possible, build in flexibility to allow staff to cover for each other.
- Draw up a list of suitable supply staff.
- Make it clear to everyone that it is quite unacceptable for individual pupils to be sent home if their supporter is away.

While it is widely accepted that LSAs and support teachers play a central role in meeting the.special needs of individual children, relatively little thought has been given to the changes that may occur in the dynamics of the classroom when a second adult moves into the class teacher's domain. Anecdotal evidence suggests that rather than being a universal boon, an additional adult can in fact be a burden to the class teacher if proper thought is not given to planning and developing teamwork. Instead of freeing up the teacher to spend more time with individual pupils, additional in-class support can mean that the hard-pressed teacher has yet one more thing to worry about.

At the same time, the presence of paid supporters can lead to children with high-level support needs being segregated within the classroom. In some instances, the presence of a supporter who has worked with the child for some time or who has acknowledged expertise, can serve to alienate class teachers who may already be doubting their ability to include a particular pupil in their lessons. One real danger is that the class or subject teacher will play 'host' to the child with SEN and their supporters and take little if any responsibility for their learning. Recent research on children with Down's Syndrome in mainstream settings (Lorenz 1999a) indicated that a significant proportion of these pupils receive little if any direct teaching from class or subject teachers. Instead, the onus for differentiation, delivery and evaluation of learning programmes was left with an often unqualified assistant.

If schools are to become more inclusive, it is essential that support is used to increase participation not reduce it. As SENCO you need to decide whether support staff are more appropriately allocated to individual pupils or are expected to work flexibly across the whole class (see Table 6.2). Even where members of staff have been appointed specifically to support a named pupil, it should be possible, if you think it appropriate, to redefine their role to promote the student's independence.

TEACHING ASSISTANT OR PERSONAL ASSISTANT

Teaching assistant	
Advantages for the child: More opportunity to participate in class activities. More opportunity to interact with friends. Choice of adults to approach for help or support. Regular contact with class teacher.	**Disadvantages:** Too many people to relate to. Low level of specialist skills. Little consistency of response across supporters. Limited knowledge and understanding of individual needs.
Advantages for the teacher: Opportunity to develop long-term partnership with LSA. Support across the whole class. More opportunity to work directly with SEN pupils. Greater flexibility of response possible.	**Disadvantages:** Most supporters lack specialist skills required to support child. Need for teacher to plan for child and differentiate curriculum. Neither partner has in-depth knowledge of child.
Advantages for the assistant: More variety in work. Opportunity to develop closer relationship with teacher. More involvement in curriculum. Higher status.	**Disadvantages:** No opportunity to develop personal relationship with child. Doing teacher's job on the cheap. Unable to support children with high-level support needs adequately.
Personal assistant	
Advantages for the child: Fewer people to relate to. High level of specialist skills. Consistency of response. Knowledge and understanding of individual needs.	**Disadvantages:** Can act as barrier between child and teacher. Can create adult dependency. Can inhibit friendships. Can segregate child within classroom.
Advantages for the teacher: Access to specialist skills and knowledge. Can concentrate on others in class. Less need to differentiate or modify for individual child. Can rely on assistant to advocate for child.	**Disadvantages:** Assistant moves on with child. No help with rest of class. Can be alienated and prevented from interacting with child. Little flexibility of response.
Advantages for the assistant: Chance to develop personal relationship with child. Role quite distinct from that of teacher. Opportunity to develop specialist skills and knowledge. Regular contact with parents.	**Disadvantages:** Can get over-involved with child. Very stressful and demanding unless job is shared. Need to develop new partnerships with teachers on regular basis. Low status as carer.

Table 6.2 The roles of teaching and personal assistants – advantages and disadvantages

There is no doubt that good partnerships between teachers and supporters are often more effective in promoting inclusion than those between supporters and children. Certainly this is the view promoted by the DfEE in their recent guidance on working with teaching assistants (DfEE 2001a). On the other hand, the Alliance for Inclusive Education (AIE 2001) points out that young people with high-level support needs rely on building a long-term relationship with one or two assistants who are 'committed to learning everything they can about the needs of the young person they work with, including knowing when to interfere and when not to'.

Schools should make sure that all support staff have:

- a clear job description which is regularly reviewed and updated
- a team leader or line manager with whom they can share concerns
- time to plan and liaise with class or subject teachers
- time to prepare or modify teaching resources
- access to appraisal or performance management
- opportunities for training.

Doyle and Lee (2000) give the following ten tips to teachers working with 'paraprofessionals':

1. Welcome them to your classroom.
2. Establish their importance as a team member.
3. Clarify their roles and responsibilities.
4. Establish shared expectations for student learning and management.
5. Ensure that they are guided by a qualified teacher.
6. Review their activities regularly.
7. Establish procedures for unexpected situations.
8. Ensure that they promote student responsibility.
9. Establish times and ways to communicate.
10. Evaluate their effectiveness in supporting learning and inclusion.

Think about issuing guidance for teaching colleagues on the use of support staff. If appropriate, consider incorporating this into a more general SEN handbook on practical ways of promoting inclusion. Suggest that part of a training day is set aside to explore issues around support. Encourage teachers and supporters to discuss ways in which they can help each other do their job better (Balshaw 1999). One common complaint (Lee and Henkhuzens 1996) is that LSAs never know what is going to be taught in a particular lesson far enough ahead to plan effectively. Where supporters are working with a number of different teachers, suggest staff issue supporters with termly lesson plans. If a single teacher and LSA work together regularly, encourage them to set aside a regular weekly slot to share the teacher's planning for the coming week and discuss ways in which it might be differentiated to meet the needs of individual pupils.

Finally, in reviewing your support systems it is important not to forget to consult the consumers. Some young people resent being singled out by obvious support; others have come to believe that they can do nothing without it. Young people generally have very clear ideas about the type of support they want and need and it is important that we listen to what they have to say. As one student quoted by Wilson and Jade (1999) comments: 'One of my assistants is dreadful. I went to the Head of Special Needs last year and said "I can't work with this woman. I'll swap her for someone else. Give her to another kid".'

Annual reviews, IEPs and target setting

> Each year students parents and professionals go through countless months of getting to know one another. Many students with disabilities go through months of being misunderstood each school year while professionals struggle to acquire an understanding of who they truly are, only for the student to move on to another set of educators the following year where the process starts all over again (Ashley's mom 2001).

So what goes wrong and how can you, as SENCO, minimise difficulties faced by children with special needs as they move through the school and maximise their inclusion?

Your first task is to make sure that each child's statement is accurate and up to date, reflecting the pupil's current needs and the provision to meet them. Too often statements are written and then ignored until the child moves school or the LEA wants to cut the level of resourcing. Use the pupil's annual review to take a thorough look at the statement in conjunction with teaching colleagues, the child's support workers, relevant outside professionals, the parents and the child. Pay particular attention to Section 3 and discuss the impact of any special arrangements on the pupil's participation in the curriculum and the life of the school.

- Too much emphasis on structured programmes of work can mean the child is taught separately from their peers for much of the day.
- Too much individual teaching or therapy can mean that the child is regularly withdrawn from lessons and, as a consequence, finds it hard to join in on their return to the classroom.
- Too much one-to-one support can act as a barrier between the pupil and their class teacher or their peers.
- Keeping children down or sending them to join a younger class for literacy or numeracy can mean that they become isolated from their friends.

- Disapplying them from parts of the curriculum can deny them opportunities to develop new skills.

If these are a major feature of the statement, discuss ways that support and therapy could be delivered as an integral part of the class curriculum and suggest that the statement is amended accordingly.

Ensure that any special arrangements or additional resources the child does require are specified and quantified.

- How many hours of LSA or support teacher time should be available for differentiating teaching materials and joint planning with class or subject teachers, as well as for in-class support? What special qualifications or training do these people need?
- How often should the pupil receive input from a qualified speech and language therapist or other outside professional for assessment, programme planning and staff training, as well as for direct therapy?
- What supplementary aids and equipment does the child need to allow them to access the curriculum?

If you are to become more inclusive it is essential that you have the right tools.

While the statement provides a framework for inclusion, it is the IEP which should be your working document. However, a recent survey of SENCOs (DfEE 1998b) indicated that many were 'uncertain about who should be involved in IEP formulation, what sort of targets were appropriate, how much detail should be included in IEPs, how often they should be updated and how to monitor their implementation'. An IEP must be a user-friendly document which is meaningful to everyone who works with the pupil, be they class or subject teachers, LSAs, support teachers or visiting therapists. The purpose of the IEP should be to ensure that the child's programme is coordinated and that everyone is working towards the same goals. For this reason it is important that all those involved feel some ownership of the document and have contributed to its creation. This must also include the parents and the young people themselves.

The most important aspect of any IEP is the section which specifies the outcomes to be achieved by the next IEP review. Too often IEPs focus almost exclusively on the acquisition of basic skills or the eradication of inappropriate behaviours, rather than on the development of the pupil as a whole. In too many instances targets are still not SMART, i.e. Specific, Measurable, Achievable, Relevant and Timed. Where children have a complexity of needs, schools often try to cover the entire curriculum within a single IEP, rather than focus on a small number of key areas.

To ensure that IEPs are manageable yet address the central issues of inclusion, it is recommended that you follow the procedure below:

1. At the Annual Review meeting discuss the child's current level of functioning under the following headings:
   COMMUNICATION
   MOBILITY AND COORDINATION
   LITERACY AND NUMERACY
   CURRICULUM ACCESS
   SOCIAL SKILLS
   AGE-APPROPRIATE BEHAVIOUR
   INDEPENDENCE
   PARTICIPATION IN SCHOOL LIFE
2. Agree the progress the pupil might be expected to make in each area during the following year and set annual goals. Place these in priority order.
3. After the meeting draw up no more than six specific targets, one from each of the priority areas, and share these with the student, their parents and anyone else directly involved. Encourage them to suggest ways in which these could best be achieved and incorporate them into an IEP (see Tables 6.3 and 6.4).

   Generally it is recommended that schools devise their own IEPs rather than use a standard format. Even then, you may find that the IEPs you use for pupils at earlier stages are not particularly helpful for pupils with statements and complex needs. Those of you working in the secondary sector may also feel that subject teachers need the opportunity to modify the IEP or supplement it with a subject specific action plan that better meets the demands of their subject area.

Name: Sam Jameson.	Class: 8 Blue.		Date: September 2001.
Teaching objective:	Class activity:	Intervention strategy:	Success criteria:
Communication To ask for own dinner at canteen.	Lunchtime – selecting own meal.	Lunchtime supervisor to prompt then wait at least 1 minute.	Verbalises choice within given time four days out of five.
Numeracy To be able to count on (in head) using digits 1–10.	Maths lesson (middle set with two teachers).	Teacher to work individually with Sam within classroom on strategy.	To be able to use counting on (in head) for completing addition sums.
Social skills To come to school on bus with friends.	Coming to school.	Friends to call for Sam on way to bus stop.	Comes into school with friends nine days out of ten.
Independence To complete six lines of free writing, seeking peer support when required.	History lesson. (Pupils discussing topic in small groups then writing up own account.)	LSA to go over topic discussed and record main ideas, plus key words. Then to move away and work with others until task completed.	Six lines completed without adult help in two lessons out of three.

Table 6.3 Example of an IEP

Name: Sarah Palmer.	Class: 3.		Date: September 2001.
Teaching objective:	Class activity:	Intervention strategy:	Success criteria:
Literacy To read Book 5 of reading scheme.	Literacy hour.	LSA to teach words from book on flash cards, with group of peers, before book introduced.	To read Book 5 to teacher with 90% accuracy.
Independence To be able to dress herself after PE, including buttons and zips, within 10–15 minutes.	Getting dressed after games and PE.	To be asked to get dressed 5 minutes before peers. Practical help from LSA to be gradually reduced. Praise for speed.	Successfully dressed, including fastenings, with minimal help. Back in class with peers three times out of five.
Inclusion To play shepherd in nativity play.	Christmas play. All Year 3 children involved.	To be given lots of time to practise lines. Friend to stand beside her.	To perform in play in public and to remember lines.

Table 6.4 Another example of an IEP

4. Ensure that all IEPs are monitored at least twice a year and targets updated. Involve the student as fully as you can in the review process and take note of their views. Strategies that are not working should be modified and successes celebrated with the parents, the child and the whole school community
5. To accompany the IEP, consider working with the parents and the child on a student profile that will put the flesh on the bones of the IEP (Ashley's mom 2001). Include things the child enjoys doing, ways in which they communicate their feelings and how they can be helped to cope with difficulties.
6. Always remember that behind the statement and the IEP is a young person whose greatest need is to be accepted for who they are and to be valued for what they can contribute to the life of your school.

Chapter 7

First Steps for Class Teachers

Reviewing the situation

> Dear Teacher,
>
> You just found out that a student with disabilities is being placed in your classroom ... Don't panic! My guess is that you already know much of what you need to for this to be a successful experience for you and your class; it's a matter of applying the knowledge and skills you already possess to a new situation. It's been done before by other teachers, and you can do it too.

So begins the first of the *Quick Guides to Inclusion* by Giangreco (1997) If you find yourself in just such a position, as a class teacher at primary level or as a subject teacher in the secondary sector, this chapter is for you. Its aim is to help you think about some of the issues you will need to address and provide you with some ideas on a positive way forward. Classroom teachers hold the keys to inclusion. At this point in time you may have considerable doubts about your ability to reach and teach a student with significant disabilities in your classroom. However, you will find, as many have before you, that inclusion draws on just the same skills as were required to make you a good teacher in the first place.

As O'Brien and Forest (1998) note, all good teachers:

1. Respond to individual differences among students by adapting curricula and routines.
2. Involve all students in class work by using a variety of instructional methods.
3. Create a safe environment that encourages responsible, cooperative behaviour.
4. Collaborate and share tasks effectively with teaching assistants.
5. Make good use of resource people without giving up responsibility for the class.
6. Build networks with colleagues to provide mutual help and support.
7. Increase their own repertoire of skills and abilities.

Once you know that you will be having a student with a disability in your classroom, your first job is to see beyond the label that is tied around their neck. Many teachers waste a great deal of time reading extensively about 'autism' or 'cerebral palsy' only to find that the child who eventually reaches their classroom is nothing like the examples described in the textbooks. Many books are out of date or provide a medically focused or negative picture. While there are some excellent resources on the market, it is always better to wait until you know the individual child before consulting them.

If the child already attends your school, it is probably more useful to talk to colleagues about their experiences so far. Ask them to tell you about their successes and what approaches have worked particularly well, not just about what went wrong or about the child's shortcomings. Ideally, they should be prepared to summarise this information in the form of a student profile (see Figure 7.1) which will give you a lot of useful information. However, never forget that children behave differently in different settings and with different people, so don't assume that you will face exactly the same challenges as your colleagues. Nevertheless, their comments will provide a useful starting point for your planning. If the student is new to your school, try to visit their previous placement and if possible observe the child there as well as talking to staff.

Name of student:	Date:
1. What are some of their strengths?	
2. In what areas have they shown most progress?	
3. What are some of their favourite school activities?	
4. What do they find motivating? How do you know?	
5. What do they find reinforcing?	
6. What are some of the ways they participate in the class curriculum?	
7. What teaching strategies have worked well in the past?	
8. What teaching strategies have not worked well?	
9. What type of LSA support has been most effective?	
10. Who are their friends? What do they do together in school or outside?	

Figure 7.1 Student profile (adapted from Doyle (1997))

If you are in a primary school, the next step is to invite the parents in for a chat, ideally well before the child starts in your class. Alternatively, offer to do a home visit if they prefer. The aim of this initial session is twofold. First, it should serve to reassure the parents that you are keen to welcome their child into your class and do what you can to make their time with you as happy and productive as you can make it. Secondly, it should give you the opportunity to listen to the parents and learn what you can from them to enable you to do your job better. Ask the family if they mind you making notes as they talk as this will help you in your planning.

If you are in a secondary school, it will clearly not be possible for each teacher to meet with the parents individually, but it would be useful to invite them into school to meet with a group of staff who will be working with their child in the coming year. If they are new to the school and feel anxious about meeting a number of new faces, ask your SENCO to suggest they are accompanied by a representative from an appropriate voluntary agency, the school educational psychologist or someone from their primary school.

Having gathered information from people who know the child well, your next task is to get to know the individual student. If they are already attending your school, it should be quite possible for you to spend time chatting to them and their friends informally. Suggest to their current class teacher or form tutor that you talk to the whole class about the ways in which your class will be different from their present one. Suggest that some of the new skills they will need are introduced to the whole class before they move up.

If they are coming from a preschool setting or from another school, try to make a series of visits so they get to know you and you them. Make sure they have the opportunity to visit your school with classmates as part of the normal transfer process, but supplement this, if possible, by extra visits. If they are transferring on their own, arrange for them to visit at the same time as pupils from a feeder school who will be starting with you at the same time. This will ensure that there are at least a few familiar faces on their first day.

In the first few weeks:

- Spend time getting to know the child before making any modifications to the classroom or the curriculum.
- Encourage them to take part in all aspects of classroom and school life, initially with minimal support, but observe where they are having problems.
- Identify any special skills you will need in order to work with them effectively.
- Talk to therapists or other professionals who may be available to support you or the child and discuss their involvement.
- Spend time with any teaching assistants appointed to support the child and discuss how best they might promote inclusion.
- If you will be working with the same asssistant regularly, try to set up a schedule of meetings for planning and feedback.
- Finally, meet with the SENCO to discuss IEP goals, additional resources, differentiation, training or anything else that is causing you concern.

Teaching and learning

> The challenge for teachers of children with limited academic, physical or other abilities is to provide an education that allows them participation in a meaningful and relevant way. Using a variety of strategies, support people and physical resources is usually more successful than simply providing a special program in the same room or a separate program in another room (Lang and Berberich 1995).

As Lang and Berberich note, children learn best in a setting where they:

- find a sense of belonging and acceptance
- are valued for their individual gifts and the contribution they make
- are offered choices and take responsibility for their own learning
- have fun and enjoy what they are doing
- feel safe to take risks and respond to challenges.

The process of differentiating the curriculum to accommodate a student with significant disabilities is to all extents and purposes the same as you would normally use. However, you will need to think about it rather more carefully and take account of the student's individual learning style. Differentiation can take many forms (see Figure 7.2).

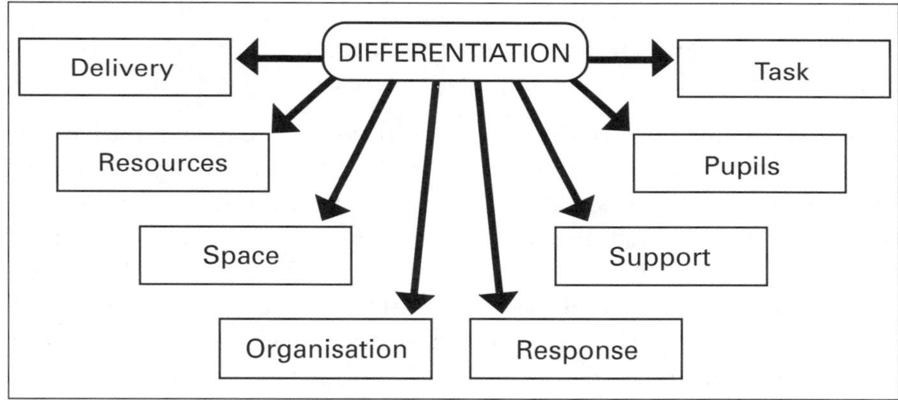

Figure 7.2 The many forms of differentiation

It may be necessary to alter the way you present new information or teach a new skill. In deciding the most appropriate form of delivery to use you need to be aware of the child's

- hearing levels
- comprehension level
- auditory memory
- visual acuity
- visual memory
- personal interests
- previous experience.

As a consequence, you may need:

- to give additional visual support, using pictures or real objects
- to simplify your language or use shorter sentences
- to present material in smaller chunks
- to repeat instructions during the session
- to pay particular attention to linking new learning to prior experiences
- to demonstrate or ask a peer to model appropriate procedures.

In some cases it may be appropriate to follow more general class instruction with a short session of direct instruction where the student is supported on a one-to-one basis, has the task broken down into smaller steps and is then guided through each step by you or the child's LSA. Hopefully, once the child has grasped the basics of the task, they should be able to return to working in a group with a lower level of support.

In selecting appropriate tasks for a disabled child to complete, there is no need to design a separate menu of activities. Instead look at what the rest of the class are being asked to do and select those activities which:

- are matched to the child's ability, but provide a measure of challenge
- can be completed independently or with minimal support
- are matched to the child's interests
- offer variety and choice and lead to different outputs
- are graded to build new skills and increase confidence.

Not only can you increase opportunities for learning by careful selection of tasks, but you can also build success by changing expected outcomes. Instead of writing, let the student respond orally to you or a peer. Let them draw pictures and attach pre-written sticky labels. Encourage the use of photographs, tape recordings or storyboards. Differentiation of resources is clearly essential if maximum participation is to be achieved. A well-prepared student with relevant resources at hand should be able to learn independently. On the other hand, where preparation has been poor, teaching materials are inappropriate and there is little supportive equipment or technology, disabled students will have no choice but to rely heavily on support staff.

Look at your classroom and check that:

- reading matter is at an appropriate readability level and worksheets are suitable
- dictionaries and study guides are accessible and the student knows how to use them
- the student with writing difficulties has access to alternative forms of record-keeping
- supportive technology is available in the classroom
- lists of key words have been produced for each subject area.

Finally, think about how you use space and furniture in your classroom, how you group pupils and how you use support. All are critical if you are to maximise inclusion for disabled students.

In organising your curriculum delivery, think about ways of maximising the participation of the disabled student as advocated by Giangreco and his colleagues in their COACH programme (Giangreco *et al.* 1998). Where the young person can participate in the normal class activity and pursue the same goals as their peers, make sure that they do so. If this presents insurmountable challenges, consider 'multilevel instruction' whereby all students in the class pursue goals within the same topic or programme of study, but at different levels. Alternatively think about a system of 'curriculum overlapping' whereby the student participates in the class lesson, but is actually pursuing objectives from another curriculum area. Thus in science, the learning disabled student might be pursuing a maths goal of developing one-to-one correspondence by giving out and collecting in equipment, or a language goal by joining in a group discussion.

On occasions, it may be necessary for students to pursue alternative activities if:

- the lesson offers no opportunity for them to pursue appropriate goals, e.g. during a written test
- the student needs experiences not available in the ordinary classroom, e.g. mobility training or a structured articulation programme
- medical or personal management needs have to be met in privacy, e.g. postural drainage or catheterisation
- the student is becoming restless and needs a short break from the set tasks.

When designing individualised programmes make sure that:

- targets are clearly stated and sessions kept short with the child rejoining their peers as soon as possible
- individual sessions focus on skills the child will need to access the class curriculum or are used to consolidate learning or prepare for lessons later in the day
- other children are included wherever possible (in some schools pupils with marked difficulties may join a younger class for a particular activity, rather than being taught on their own)
- children are encouraged to start any new activity with the class (only when they are clearly struggling or becoming restless should they be offered an alternative)
- withdrawal is seen not as a punishment for being naughty, but as a positive choice.

Using the peer group to best effect

In reviewing the resources at your disposal to promote the inclusion of a student with significant disabilities, it is important that you don't forget the value of involving other young people. As O'Brien and Forest (1998) comment: 'Students create opportunities for one another to collaborate and grow. Without the resources they bring individually and as a group, inclusion is impossible.'

On taking on a new teaching group containing a child with disabilities, your first task is to begin developing a feeling of community in the classroom, whereby students trust and support each other. This is particularly important if the group has not worked together before or if there are new children in the class. From the beginning you need to set the tone and build a culture of mutuality. Students should feel the class belongs to them, not just to you.

- Model the language of cooperation and show respect for others in the way you interact with your students, with other members of staff and with parents.
- Consult your students on how the room should be set up and discuss with them what special arrangements might be required to accommodate the student with disabilities.
- Take time to agree class rules and routines. Set aside regular sessions for whole-class discussions and explore ways in which students can help each other deal with unwelcome behaviours such as bullying.
- Give students opportunities to get to know each other and talk with their friends. Make it clear that you believe positive relationships to be as important as good work.
- Build a programme of disability awareness into your curriculum. Rather than focusing on the specific disability of one student, explore the whole range of disabilities. Help your class understand that disability is just a part of life, not something to be ashamed of.
- Think about using circle time as part of your weekly programme. Formal circle time sessions at primary (Curry and Broomfield 1994) or secondary level (Moseley and Tew 1999) can be extremely useful in developing a whole range of relevant skills that build positive relationships (see Figure 7.3).

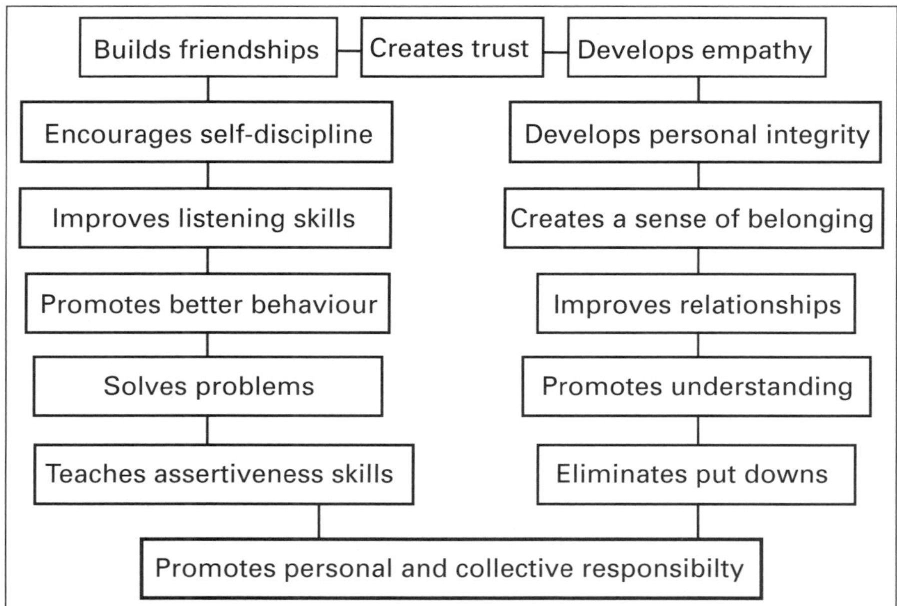

Figure 7.3 Circle time (after Moseley and Tew 1999)

To supplement whole-class discussions, you might wish to consider setting up a circle of friends for a particular student, especially if they are having a hard time in school. This approach (Wilson and Newton 1999) allows a self-selected group of peers to problem-solve around the issues faced by a single individual. Generally, whole-class circle time seems to work best with younger children and a more focused circle of friends with older ones. However, if you are interested, read the books, find some allies and have a go.

If you are prepared to commit the time, the benefits will almost certainly outweigh the disadvantages. A group of supportive peers can be of value not only in increasing social participation in school but in involving the disabled student in out-of-school activities. They can also provide useful insights which can inform the IEP and the student's annual review. While pupils are increasingly being invited to participate in their own reviews it is as yet rare to find their friends being involved as well. Maybe you could be the first person in your school or your district to encourage peer involvement in planning and review meetings.

As Gross (2000) notes, we must never forget that for most children, interaction with the peer group is the most important thing that happens at school, and work with a peer a more powerful energiser than even the most inspiring teaching. So in organising your classroom to include a child with significant disabilities, think about creating opportunities for children to work together. In developing group work, as Marvin (1998) points out, the size and composition of the group can be crucial in its success or failure.

Research suggests that groups of four are generally the most effective, but in the early stages of group development it may be better for students to work in pairs initially. Hittie (2000) uses a system he calls 'clock partners' in his primary classroom in Michigan. Each student has a chart with a large clock face on it. Students ask each other to sign on each hour line. They cannot ask anyone twice and no one who is asked can refuse. Activities are then set and students requested to complete them with their 7 o'clock or their 3 o'clock partner. If necessary, students working with a disabled peer can be given guidance on how to adapt the task to involve their partner. However, such interventions are rarely needed as young people are surprisingly good at making the requisite modifications.

A rather different approach to partner work can be found in the extensive literature on peer support and peer tutoring (Foot *et al.* 1990). Here students are selected in such a way that one partner acts as a teacher and the other as a learner. Tutors can come from the same class, a parallel class or an older age group and are specifically trained in their role. Not only do children being coached by a peer learn at least as well if not better than those taught by an adult, the peer tutor also gains in skills and confidence.

One perceived drawback of peer tutoring is that the more able partner may dominate the relationship and inhibit productive interaction. Research on pairs and groups has shown that in order to promote positive attitudes, raise self-esteem and promote effective learning, all pupils should be given the opportunity to act as tutor to a peer with a lower level of skill. Look at the disabled student in your class and identify an area of strength or a particular ability which they might impart to a peer or a child from lower down the school.

In developing collaborative group work, it is often best to begin with small practical activities where there is a specific and achievable solution within the joint capabilities of the group. Over time, the tasks can become more complex providing valuable opportunities for discussion and debate. Input from you or your LSA can be useful in promoting the social skills required for cooperation and providing necessary prompts to move the students on. However, it is important for you to know when to stand back and allow the students to resolve problems themselves.

Wherever possible, students should be encouraged to work in mixed ability settings. Research, quoted by Marvin (1998), has shown that the majority of students make most progress both academically and socially in such groupings. For group work to be effective, it is essential to plan the tasks carefully so that each group member:

- is actively involved
- is working at an appropriate level
- is able to contribute something of value to the group
- is aware of their role and the purpose of their task.

One commonly used approach is termed 'jigsawing' and involves the teacher breaking the group task down into smaller interdependent parts which can be completed by individuals or smaller groups and then combined to form a joint outcome.

At Southfield School, the Year 6 teacher decided to divide the class into mixed ability groups to produce story books for the nursery. Each group consisted of a story teller, a scribe, an artist and a bookbinder. Everyone wanted James, a young man with learning difficulties, in their group as he had the wildest imagination and told the most fantastic stories. Each group produced their book and even though James couldn't write or draw beautiful pictures, his stories were voted the best in the class.

Building a support network

There is little doubt that working in the area of inclusion is both professionally demanding and emotionally draining. As Lang and Berberich (1995) note, class teachers often struggle to come to some sort of understanding of how they feel about having children with extreme special needs in their classroom. The conflict between trying to treat the child 'normally' and making allowances for their special needs can lead to frustration and feelings of helplessness.

Without guidance, teachers are often uncertain about what constitutes satisfactory progress. Many teachers who are doing an excellent job feel that they are failing because no one is there to give them the reassurance and recognition they deserve. The practicalities of inclusion lead many teachers to feel inadequately supported. The presence of a well-trained LSA, while no panacea, can take a lot of pressure off the overworked class teacher. Similarly, a head teacher who understands how much extra work is involved and provides regular planning and preparation time can make a tremendous difference to teacher morale and wellbeing.

So what sorts of supports should you as a class teacher in an inclusive school be looking for? For many teachers, the answer to the pressures of inclusion is to seek solutions from experts. However as one teacher quoted by Tashie *et al.* (1993) commented: 'I really appreciate all the support, but sometimes there are so many adults in my classroom, it feels like a cocktail party. I wonder if I should be teaching or serving hors d'oeuvres.'

While input from outside specialists can be valuable, your first port of call should always be your own school. In the primary school, a committed head teacher should be aware of the additional demands placed on a class teacher trying to do their best for a child with significant disabilities. Sadly this is not always the case and so you may have an education job to do.

(a) Invite the head teacher to observe your class at work or suggest that they might like to take the class themselves while you prepare teaching materials or work elsewhere in the school.
(b) Discuss the level of in-class support currently available and the way in which it is being used. If necessary, enlist their help in approaching the LEA or the school governors for additional resources.
(c) Make them aware of the importance of joint planning with your LSA and discuss ways in which timetables could be adjusted or time released.
(d) Discuss any training requirements you or your LSA might have and negotiate ways in which these could be met.
(e) Share any concerns you have about assessment and discuss how best the child should be involved in SATs or school-based tests and examinations.

In some primary schools and most secondaries, it may not be possible or appropriate for you to approach the head teacher directly. However, it is important that you obtain both practical and emotional support from the SMT. In many schools this is best achieved via the SENCO who should be fully aware of the problems you face.

(a) Arrange to meet with your SENCO on a regular basis to discuss the child's progress and participation in classroom activities. Seek help and advice on differentiating the curriculum and implementing IEP targets.

(b) If they have the time, invite them to team teach with you and demonstrate alternative strategies to overcome identified difficulties and maximise participation. Show you value their expertise and are willing to learn.
(c) Discuss the role of LSAs, and share any concerns you may have about their work or the way they are being managed. Ask your SENCO to act as an arbitrator if there are problems you cannot resolve yourself.
(d) With their support, plan any necessary behavioural interventions and discuss the possible involvement of an LEA behaviour support teacher or educational psychologist.
(e) As class teacher or form tutor, make sure you are invited to any meeting or review that they arrange. However tempting it may be to hand over responsibility for aspects of the student's programme, you will not be successful unless you remain involved.

The third source of support in school should be your teaching colleagues. While they are undoubtedly feeling just as overworked and stressed out as you are, it is vital that you support each other and share your worries.

(a) Seek out a group of supportive colleagues who will agree to meet on a regular basis to discuss students causing concern. Use them as a sounding board and pool problem-solving strategies.
(b) Share your planning with a colleague within the same Key Stage or subject area and discuss ways in which you might differentiate the programme for particular students.
(c) Consider sharing the responsibility for the disabled student. Think about team teaching across two classes or regrouping pupils from both classes for specific topics, allowing you both to teach all the children at different times.
(d) Suggest that one staff meeting a term is devoted to discussing pupils with significant disabilities. At these sessions, share successes and seek support from the whole staff in resolving ongoing problems. Make it clear that inclusion is a whole-school issue, not just the responsibility of this year's teachers.
(e) Involve colleagues in including your disabled student in clubs or out-of-school activities with which they are connected. Encourage as many people as possible to get to know the student and view them in a positive light.

The fourth source of support is your teaching assistant or LSA. Remember that they are there just as much to support you as to support the individual child.

(a) Treat them with respect and consideration at all times. Make it clear that you value their contribution and their friendship.
(b) Share the load by planning together on a weekly basis and encouraging regular feedback and suggestions.

(c) Encourage them to supervise the whole class once they are engaged in a set activity, enabling you to work with the individual student or a small group.
(d) Show them how to carry out a structured observation or complete recording sheets, freeing you from the sole responsibility for data collection.
(e) Provide guidance on the differentiation of future lessons and then release your LSA to prepare teaching materials at times when you are happy to manage the whole class on your own.

The fifth source of support available on a daily basis is the child's parents. They have a major investment in the successful inclusion of their child and in the majority of cases will do anything they can to support you.

(a) Communicate with them regularly in person or via a home/school book. Highlight successes and boost their confidence in your ability to meet their child's needs.
(b) Share concerns with them at an early stage and problem-solve together. Make it clear that you are not trying to get rid of their child or send them to a special school.
(c) Enlist their help in providing additional teaching materials or equipment. Most parents are only too willing to contribute if they know what you need.
(d) Ask them to teach you about their child's disability and lend you any relevant books. They will almost certainly be very well informed and happy to pass on their knowledge.
(e) If they have the time, ask them to help out on school trips or when staffing is an issue. Be honest with them about any problems you envisage and value the help they can offer.

Finally, make sure you enlist the support of your whole class. They probably know more than any adult about the problems faced by the disabled child and what to do about them. Never forget that they are your best allies.

Chapter 8

First Steps for Learning Supporters

Clarifying the supporter's role

If you are a support assistant or nursery nurse with particular responsibility for supporting one or more named children with significant disabilities in a mainstream school, this chapter is written particularly for you. It doesn't matter whether you are called a special needs assistant, an inclusion assistant, a special support assistant or a teaching assistant – the issues are just the same. Some of you may have been in the same school for a number of years and suddenly be asked to work with a child with a disability you have never encountered before. Others will have been appointed specifically to support a named child. Whatever the case, the most important thing is for you to be clear about why you are there.

Traditionally, the concept of special needs support in mainstream schools was based on the belief that children with significant disabilities were in some way different from ordinary children. Since they had 'special educational needs' they obviously needed something special or extra, as in a special school. As a consequence, the emphasis was on the provision of individual structured programmes designed by specialists to overcome their deficits. As these bore little relation to what the rest of the class was doing, they were usually delivered on a one-to-one basis by a supporter at the back of the class, in a support base, in the corridor or in the staffroom.

At the same time, considerable attention has always been paid to meeting the medical and physical needs of the child. Supporters have been expected to push wheelchairs, carry out physiotherapy programmes, change colostomy bags, administer medication, dress, feed and toilet their charges. Above all the aim has been to keep these vulnerable children safe, while at the same time protecting schools from possible complaints from parents or outside agencies. Sadly, one outcome of this approach has been to create young people who can do little for themselves and who expect their 'personal slave' to be at hand whenever things get difficult.

The ultimate aim of these interventions was to change the child in some way to enable them to fit better into the existing system. This process was termed 'integration'. Since few people believed that children with significant difficulties were able to take part in ordinary lessons, no one worried about the amount of time that they were working on their own with an adult or were withdrawn from the classroom for individual programmes or therapy. Few teachers had developed the skills required to differentiate the curriculum for these children and fewer still had realised the importance of more able peers in providing good role models and raising expectations. Children who were eager to help their disabled peers were pushed away and told to get on with their own work. As a consequence, many disabled young people, while attending ordinary schools, were socially isolated and made few friends (see Figure 8.1).

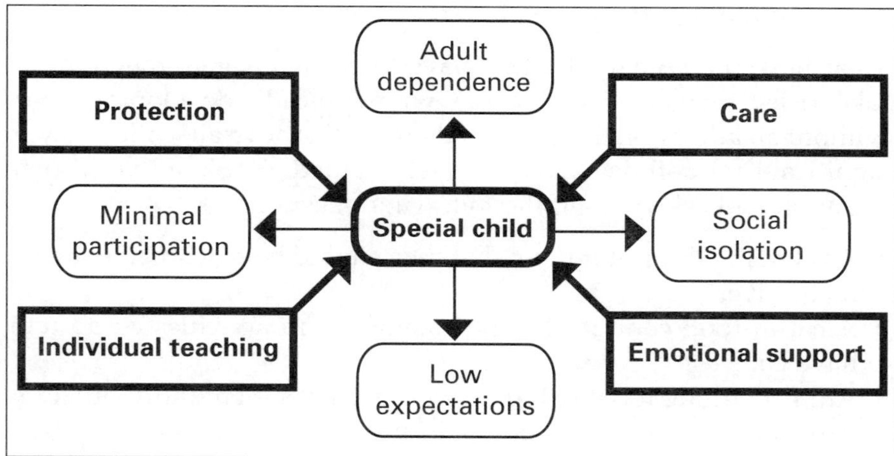

Figure 8.1 The traditional role of the supporter

> Mrs Marny was not only good at making large mistakes but little ones too. She was so nervous about leaving me that I had to accompany her to the loo! And when I first took my powered wheelchair to school in order to be more independent in the playground, she insisted on running beside me, shooing away any friend who tried to come and play with me (AIE 2001).

As time has gone on and professionals have started listening to parents and to disabled young people themselves, the emphasis has begun to change. Instead of trying to create a special school environment inside the ordinary school, people are realising that inclusion is not about overcoming deficits or about protecting young people from harm. Rather, it is about welcoming them into the school community unconditionally and enabling them to participate as fully as possible in everything that is going on. Each of us needs to feel valued for who we are and what we are able to contribute, and this applies just as much to young people with disabilities as to the rest of us.

If we want to raise children's self-esteem it is important that we don't spend our time feeling sorry for them, patronising them or expecting less of them than we do of others.. A disability does not stop a child having feelings or views as to how their needs are best met, even if we have to work hard at discovering what these are. We all need to be given choices and to exert some control over our lives. If we deny these human rights to the young people we support, then we must not be surprised if they become uncooperative or angry, taking out their frustrations on us.

Instead of trying to make young people with disabilities as 'normal' as possible, your emphasis should be on:

- boosting self-esteem
- teaching valued life skills
- developing independence
- helping build friendships
- ensuring full participation in school life.

To achieve these goals children have to be challenged; they have to take risks; they have to interact with typically developing peers without an adult breathing down their neck. Above all, children with significant disabilities have to feel wanted. Look at your own situation and ask yourself the following questions:

- Am I doing things for them that they should have learned to do for themselves?
- Am I in total control of their timetable and activities or do they have choices?
- Am I spending too much time working with them individually?
- Am I offering support that could be offered more naturally by a friend?

Once you have worked out what you think your role should be, check this out with your teaching colleagues and with the child's parents. Clearly there are going to be problems if your perceptions are different from theirs. Some teachers are very anxious about including a child with significant difficulties in their lessons and would prefer you to assume full responsibility for their learning. Others may feel uncomfortable about having another adult in the room and will prefer you to withdraw the child on a regular basis. In either case, the teacher will need as much support and encouragement from you as the child if inclusion is to be effective.

Having reached agreement, make sure your responsibilities are detailed in a comprehensive job description which is regularly updated. Examples can be found in *Working with Teaching Assistants* (DfEE 2001a), *Supporting Support Assistants* (Lorenz 1999b) and *A Handbook for Learning Support Assistants* (Fox 1998). Alongside your general job description it is useful to produce a weekly or daily schedule in conjunction with the colleagues you work with (see Table 8.1) This is particularly helpful when you are working with a number of different teachers.

Mrs Willis's Activity Timetable: Monday a.m. Year 1.		
Time	Class activity	LSA responsibilities
8.30	With friends in playground, cloakroom and classroom.	Set up classroom with teacher. Help all children with coats etc. Check Freddy's hearing aid and Amy's walking frame.
9.00	Assembly	Weekly planning meeting with teacher.
9.30	Literacy Hour	Share reading big book with teacher. Support Freddy and Amy in small group.
10.30	Break	Feedback to teacher over cup of tea.
10.45	Science	Help Amy with practical tasks as directed by teacher and physio.
11.30	PE	Support Amy in dressing herself. Encourage peers to support Amy. Once Amy is involved, return to classroom to prepare materials for afternoon session.

Table 8.1 Example of a schedule

Increasing children's independence

As a parent, one of the greatest satisfactions comes from knowing that your children have reached the point when they are able to venture out into the world without you being there to hold their hands. Good parenting should result in young people with the necessary skills and confidence to look after themselves, make their own decisions, develop and maintain relationships. Much the same criteria could be used to define good supporting. So what can you do, as a supporter, to facilitate this learning and eventually do yourself out of a job? Your first task is to help the pupils you support feel good about themselves. The 'LSA from Heaven' (AIE 2001) is always there for the young person, likes them and their friends, has a big heart, is brainy, friendly and fun.

If you are to aspire to this ideal, you must:

- be prepared to listen to and learn from young people themselves
- respect their point of view and their confidences
- develop a relationship of trust
- try always to be consistent, fair and encouraging.

As Fox (1998) notes, any child who is considered 'different' may encounter negative attitudes, particularly if their disability is obvious. You can help counter the adverse effects of such prejudice, first, by acting as an advocate for the young person and challenging negative remarks, be they from colleagues, parents or from other children, and second, by providing opportunities in which they can gain success and be seen to do so. Give them responsibilities such as taking the register to the office or giving out equipment. Finally, you can make sure that their efforts are noted and genuine achievements rewarded.

One of the problems that our current model of individual support has created is that of adult dependency. A child who has never had to put on their own coat, work through a maths problem or cut out their own model will, in time, believe that they are incapable of doing such tasks on their own. This 'learned helplessness' can then spread to other situations where, at the first sign of difficulty, the child will just give up and wait for someone to complete the task for them. If we are to encourage children to be more independent it is essential that we:

- stand back and persuade them to have a go for themselves
- give them lots of opportunities to practise and develop their skills
- reward their efforts and convince them that they can be successful.

Look at the way you currently work and what messages it gives to the children you support, to the rest of the class and to other adults (see Figure 8.2).

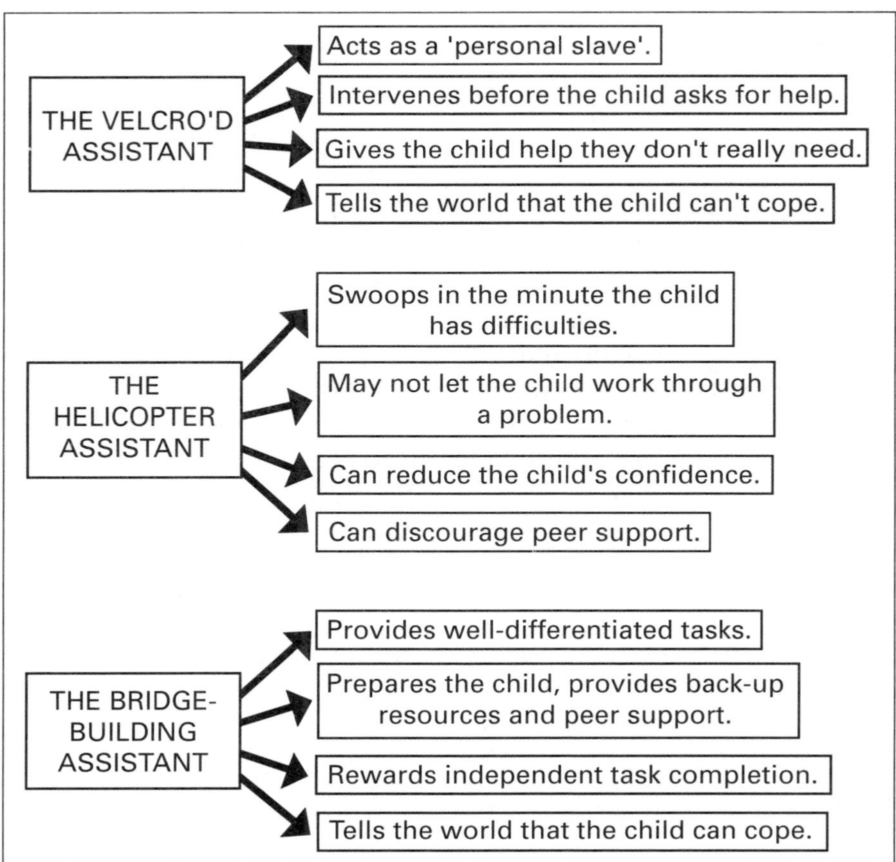

Figure 8.2 Models of support

Miranda is a 'Velcro'd' assistant. Each morning she meets Darshan and his mother in the playground. She takes him into school and hangs up his coat, then leads him by the hand into the classroom. When he sits on the carpet with his peers, she sits behind him on a small chair. When he fidgets it is Miranda who tells him off while the teacher gets on with the lesson. During lessons she is constantly at his side, prompting him when he goes off task and helping him when he gets stuck. She takes him to the toilet and stays with him at playtime in case he hurts himself or runs out into the road. If you were Miranda what might you want to do differently to increase Darshan's independence?

Jamie is a helicopter assistant with eyes in the back of his head. Although he spends part of each day working with other children in the class, Sandra is his priority and he always knows what she is up to. He is the one who explains what she is expected to do and drops what he is doing the minute she seems to be struggling. If she gets stuck she just sits quietly and waits for Jamie to come to her aid. Other children are discouraged from helping her as this is Jamie's job. Do you think this approach is helping Sandra turn into a confident and independent learner? If you were Jamie what might you want to do differently?

Delia supports Rosa but sees herself as a bridge builder. She encourages Rosa to have a go at everything her peers are doing and only ask for help when she really needs it. At the start of each lesson Delia makes sure that Rosa has all the special equipment she needs and that her teacher understands how to make the lesson accessible. As Rosa is able to cope so well on her own, Delia has time to modify teaching materials before they are needed and to consult with colleagues in the school and with visiting specialists. What do you think Rosa would be like now if Delia had been a Velcro'd assistant? Are there things you can learn from the way Delia works that might help the child you support to be more independent?

Experience suggests that some of the following approaches might be useful:

- Instead of always sitting beside your designated child, try sitting beside the teacher while the lesson is introduced. This will raise your profile and give other children the message that the disabled child is a full member of the class.
- Try never to talk over the teacher. Not only is it setting a bad example to the children but it encourages the disabled child to see you as their teacher.
- Always spend part of the day helping other children while your designated child completes a task independently, cooperates with peers or works with their class teacher.
- Teach the child you support to follow the procedure below when they face difficulties: have another try, then ask a friend, then put your hand up and ask an adult.
- Insist that the class or subject teacher disciplines the child you support in just the same way as they would the rest of the class.

- When your designated child is involved in whole-class activities, use the time to prepare resources or complete record sheets.

Finally, make sure that there are targets for developing independence on the child's IEP. On a day-to-day basis, see if you can help them:

- concentrate for longer before asking for help
- become more independent in dressing, going to the toilet or feeding themselves
- organise what they need for the next lesson or to take home
- move around school on their own or with a friend.

Above all, make them feel proud of what they have achieved and ensure that their successes are celebrated by their parents and by the whole school community.

Partnership and planning

To be an effective supporter it is essential that you see yourself as a member of a team. Around any young person with a significant disability in a mainstream school there are likely to be a large group of professionals supporting their inclusion. These people form the overall planning team, but probably only meet up once or twice a year. On a day-to-day basis, the working team around any one child is likely to be much smaller. Look at your current situation and decide who is in your team. In most primary schools in the UK, the core team often consists solely of one teacher and one supporter, but the situation can be far more complicated.

Do you share support with one or more colleagues all working with the same children at different times? To ensure continuity it is vital that you meet up regularly to compare notes and agree on your priorities and ways of working. If your timetables never coincide, talk to your SENCO about creating a half hour overlap once a week. Offer to make a small change to your hours of work or extend them slightly to allow you to meet. Alternatively, think about starting a communication book or student file in which you can keep daily records of both what you have covered and how the child or group responded. The government in its recently issued *Teaching Assistant File* (DfEE 2001b) suggests developing standard observation sheets that are quick and easy to fill in.

Do you support the same child in different classes with different teachers? While ideally you should all get together, this is rarely a realistic option. However, you can and should plan with each of them individually at least once a term. At the start of each term ask each teacher for a summary of the topics they will be covering and an outline of the type of support they would like you to offer. If you have worries about the way you are being asked to work, or about the child's learning or participation in a particular lesson, ask for a meeting with the teacher, either alone or with the SENCO, and share your concerns. Try not to criticise the teacher but share approaches that have worked in other lessons. Often a relatively brief meeting can clear the air, overcome misunderstandings and prevent similar problems occurring in the future.

One supporter quoted by Doyle (1997) illustrates this point very clearly:

> I didn't feel comfortable in the ... classroom at first because I was doing most of the 'teaching' of this young girl. Because I had no formal training in how to teach, my instructing this student just didn't seem right. The student and I became very isolated in the classroom. Sure, we were in the same room, but we were not part of the general activities. Then one day I said 'This doesn't seem right'. That was the beginning of a terrific change in my job responsibilities. The general educator (subject teacher) and I met with the special educator (SENCO) and together we shared a set of expectations. They took on the responsibility for developing the lesson plans and they started to provide the training I needed right in the classroom. In the end I learned the importance of clear, direct, honest communication.

Do you work regularly alongside a speech and language therapist or physiotherapist who leaves you activities to carry out? This can be a real problem if they never come into the classroom or talk to the class teacher. However helpful in themselves, special programmes can segregate the child from their peers and undermine your attempts to include them in the life of the class. Suggest that rather than withdrawing the child, the therapist works with you in the classroom for part of their time and involves the class teacher in any discussions.

Is your child seen regularly by a support teacher or an outreach teacher from an LEA service or special school who suggests how you should be working? This can be one of the most difficult scenarios for any supporter, as you can be pulled in two opposite directions. Ask your head teacher or SENCO to make it clear to all visiting professionals that it is the class teacher who has responsibility for the child's programme and for directing your work on a day-to-day basis. All advice should be shared initially with the class teacher who will then discuss relevant aspects with you.

Whatever your situation, it is the partnership you develop with your teacher that is the key to successful inclusion. 'By definition, support for the teacher is at the heart of the role of the teaching assistant. If a TA is not able to function well in this respect, then their ability to support pupils, curriculum and school is severely impaired' (DfEE 2001a). In developing a productive working relationship with your teacher remember that team members:

- are aware of their different but complementary roles
- respect each other's point of view
- share the same goals for pupils
- support each other in front of pupils and parents
- sort their differences out in private.

If inclusion is to be effective, it is imperative that teacher and supporter both provide input to the planning process. However well you know the child you support, remember that it is the teacher who retains responsibility for planning their learning programme. Nevertheless, there is a lot you can do to support the teacher and hence improve things for the child.

- Don't forget that the teacher may be just as apprehensive as you about getting it right and will almost certainly welcome the opportunity to learn together with a supportive but critical friend.
- Offer to look at their weekly planning and make suggestions on how activities might be modified or adapted to make them accessible.
- Discuss what special teaching materials or equipment might be useful and agree times when you can be freed up to find or make them before the relevant lesson.
- Suggest that you spend the first few minutes of the session running over the topics to be covered and any priorities the teacher has set for the child.
- Try to keep notes of key issues that can be shared at the end of the session. Make sure the teacher is kept fully informed about successes and share any worries.
- Make sure you are familiar with the way in which each teacher you work with deals with inappropriate behaviour and how this fits in with the school's behaviour policy.

As a member of staff, you have a responsibility not only to the children you support and to the teachers you work with, but to the school as a whole. Remember that: 'all adults serve as role models for pupils. Everything they do, say, respond to, and the manner in which it is done, teaches pupils about adult life' (DfEE 2001b).

Developing your own skills

'The story of learning support work … is one of dedication and hard work, of a complex job which demands diverse skills and substantial qualities of character. It is a job which is at the heart of inclusion and which has pupils and their access to learning in the mainstream at its heart' (Shaw 2001). So what qualities do you need to be an effective supporter in the inclusive classroom? Supporters in several studies have identified a whole range of personal qualities which they felt they needed to possess (see Figure 8.3). However, these alone are by no means enough if we are to include young people with significant disabilities into the life and the curriculum of mainstream schools.

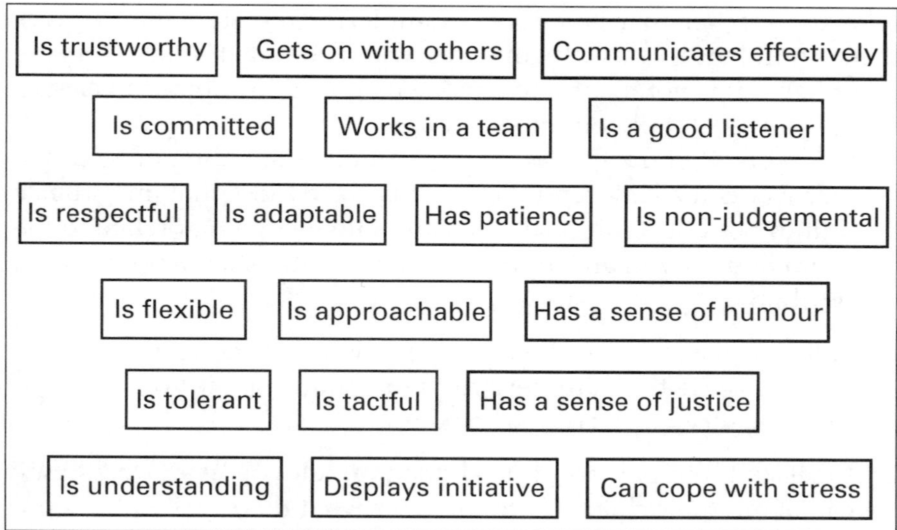

Figure 8.3 The effective supporter

So what additional skills and knowledge might you need and where can these be gained? If you are to help pupils access the curriculum you will need a good understanding of what is being taught and the methods the teacher is using. As the DfEE note (2001a), 'Assistants who are fully engaged with the aims, content, strategies and intended outcomes for a lesson are likely to be more effective than those who are required only to concentrate on individual pupils and their learning plans'.

If you work in a primary school, do you understand what goes on in the Literacy and Numeracy Hours? Do you feel comfortable in other areas of the curriculum such as science and ICT? If not:

- Ask if there are books in school you could borrow such as *Supporting Literacy and Numeracy* (Fox and Halliwell 2000).
- Ask your class teacher or the school's coordinator to talk you through the main points of their strategy one lunchtime or after school.
- Arrange to spend time practising on the class computer. Ask if you could take it home at the weekend or during holiday periods.
- Find out if there are local courses you could go on to update your knowledge. Don't worry if the courses are meant for teachers. Most course providers are happy to include keen support assistants. If not, ask if you and your class teacher could attend together.

If you work in a secondary school, don't worry if you find you don't understand everything the teachers say and you need to ask for clarification. It is useful for young people to understand that adults still find some subjects difficult and the questions you ask might help them. As one supporter quoted by Shaw (2001) notes 'Everyone in the classroom is a learner. Pupils can ask each other. I can ask the teacher, she can ask me. If you can engage in a dialogue with the teacher that is a good example for the students. It gives them confidence to ask themselves when they get stuck'. On the other hand, it is not helpful to anyone if you try to support in classes where you feel totally out of your depth.

While it is essential for you to have an understanding of what the teacher wants the children to learn, it is clearly of equal importance for you to possess additional skills and knowledge that relate to the child or children you are supporting. Before you start working with a new child:

1. Talk to teachers and supporters who worked with them previously. If they are new to your school, see if you can visit their nursery or primary school.

2. Meet with the parents and ask them to tell you as much as they can about their child. Try to discover what their expectations are for their child and how they see your role.

Find out:

- how they communicate if they don't speak clearly
- what they like doing in school and at home
- what they find most difficult and ways in which problems can be overcome
- what kinds of rewards are the best motivators
- what special skills you will need to work with them effectively.

3. Meet with the SENCO and discuss what specialised procedures you will be expected to carry out. Ask if you can be shown what to do or go on a specific training course. Sometimes therapists will come into school to train school staff or you might visit a special school where the procedures are being used.

4. Find out what you can about any specific disability the child might have. Look on the internet or consult relevant books such as *Children with Down's Syndrome* (Lorenz 1998a), *Asperger's Syndrome* (Cumine *et al.* 1998) or *Integrating Pupils with Disabilities in Mainstream Schools* (Kenward 1997).

   But remember that each of us is unique and that a disability is only one small aspect of the whole person. As one disabled young person quoted on the internet pointed out: 'A disability is the first thing other people see. Sometimes it's the only thing and then people forget to look beyond the wheelchair or the hearing aid. We don't see the person we only focus on their disability.'

   In trying to get the balance right, it might help to represent the child's needs as a thick sandwich (see Figure 8.4) where the disability is the filling. As I pointed out in *The Support Assistant's Survival Guide* (Lorenz 2001), all children, whatever their personal characteristics or disability, have the same basic need for:

- security
- a sense of identity
- to belong and feel wanted
- a sense of purpose
- achievement and success
- self-esteem.

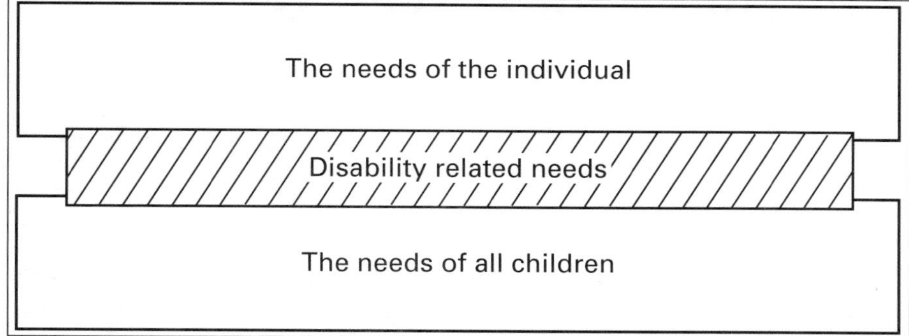

Figure 8.4 Meeting individual needs

5. Spend time with the student and get to know them and their friends. Find out what sort of help they think they need. Try not to prejudge or make assumptions about what they can do from what others have said or written about them. Start from the premise that they will take part in all class and school activities. Stand back and encourage them to join in, noting where they are experiencing difficulties.
6. Talk to the teachers you are working with and agree how best you can support the child to maximise their inclusion. Agree how and when you need to support them individually or in a group, and when you could be helping the class more generally. Look at any IEP that has already been written and help to update it using your observations. Share any additional information you have obtained and make the teacher aware of any special skills you have acquired so they can be used to best effect.

Remember that the inclusive school is a learning organisation. Don't worry if you don't know all the answers at the beginning. Don't be ashamed to ask if you are uncertain and above all listen to disabled young people and their friends – it is their lives you are trying to enhance. As you develop your role and extend your skills as a supporter, think about the comments of one young person with a significant disability (AIE 2001):

> Mrs Pen was great. She was the most adventurous of all my helpers. So many of my helpers are so scared of Health & Safety rules that they don't let me do anything in the least bit risky, but Mrs Pen realised I had to learn for myself what was safe and what wasn't . . . There were a few times when I hurt myself while with Mrs Pen . . . but I would much rather have a few broken bones and an independent life than no broken bones and a sheltered life.

Chapter 9

First Steps for Governors

Inclusion and the role of the SEN governor

As the special needs governor in a mainstream primary or secondary school you will almost certainly have heard a lot about this thing called 'inclusion'. But you are probably not very sure what it is or how it differs from 'integration'? Over the last few years there is no doubt that most ordinary schools have been taking on board increasingly challenging and complex young people. The chances are that you will now be catering for a greater number of students with statements of special educational need than ever before. Many of these young people are not significantly different from those that were previously labelled as 'slow learners' and placed in remedial classes. On the other hand, some will have far more complex needs. Traditionally these children have been 'integrated' into ordinary schools but not 'included'.

As Wilson (1998) notes, this means that:

1. They were offered their school place conditionally not as of right.
2. They could only attend as and when the school saw fit, often on a part-time basis.
3. They were often placed in classes with much younger children to avoid the need for teachers to change how or what they taught.
4. When the class work became too difficult, they would be given different work or would be withdrawn from the classroom.
5. The design and delivery of individual teaching programmes was the sole responsibility of specialists, not the class teacher.
6. Access to social activities, clubs and trips out was often limited or denied because of the problems posed to staff.
7. Overall school systems and organisation were unchanged by the presence of children with significant difficulties.

In contrast, inclusion is a process by which schools welcome and cater for an increasing diversity of students by:

1. Creating inclusive cultures and developing a secure, collaborating, stimulating community in which everyone is valued.

2. Producing inclusive policies that increase the learning and participation of all students and increase the capacity of the school to respond to pupil diversity.
3. Evolving inclusive practices within the classroom and outside it that encourage the participation of all students in the life of the school.

In thinking about the hows, whys and wherefores of inclusive education there is danger that inclusion will be seen as something that schools will get round to when they have sorted out the implications of the National Literacy Strategy, met their numeracy targets or adapted to other recent changes in our educational system. But inclusion, as Wertheimer (1997) points out, is not an add-on or the making of small adjustments to the existing system. Inclusive education involves fundamentally rethinking the meaning and purpose of education for all children and young people, a restructuring of ordinary schools. As a school governor, you have a key part to play in this process.

In your school at the moment do you have pupils who are wheelchair users, who communicate principally through sign language or read via the medium of Braille? Do you have students with learning difficulties such as Down's Syndrome, Fragile X or autism? If not, the chances are that in the near future you almost certainly will. As schools become progressively more inclusive, increasing numbers of parents of disabled children are likely to want them educated with their brothers and sisters and with non-disabled children from the local community.

The chances are that, over time, your governing body will be asked to accept a small but steadily growing number of disabled children into your school community. However, it does not mean that there will be dozens of disabled children turning up at your gates or that your standards will fall as a consequence. Most schools that prepare and plan for inclusion have seen an overall increase in school effectiveness. Morale of students and staff is raised, behaviour improves and rates of exclusion fall.

So what should you and your colleagues be doing now to promote inclusion? The responsibilities of schools which relate to pupils with SEN were laid down in the Education Act 1993 and consolidated by the Education Act 1996. The law specifies, among other duties, that the governing body of every maintained school must use its best endeavours to ensure that:

- teachers are aware of children's SEN
- the necessary provision is made for any pupil who has SEN
- children with SEN join in the activities of the school with their peers as far as is 'reasonably practicable'.

To meet these requirements, schools have traditionally been encouraged to appoint a designated SEN governor who will take a particular interest in the way the school manages its provision for children with SEN and report on this regularly to the governing body. However, the new regulations for school governors (DfEE 2000) suggest that the governing body should take a rather broader view and adopt a largely strategic role in the running of a school. Governors should, with the head teacher, decide the school's general policy and approach to meeting pupils' SEN. While the head teacher is responsible for the internal organisation, management and control of the school, the governors should act as 'critical friends'.

This approach is particularly suited to the development of inclusive education which needs to be tackled on a whole-school basis. Within the last year, all schools will have received the *Index for Inclusion* (Booth *et al.* 2000) which is designed to support schools in the process of inclusive school development. One of the problems faced by governing bodies is the need to reconcile the government's standards agenda, whereby all schools are expected to set and meet ever-more demanding academic targets, with their expressed wish to promote a more inclusive school system. What the index offers is a systematic approach to school development that aims to further inclusion and at the same time promote achievement.

Have you and your fellow governors seen and discussed the *Index for Inclusion*?

- If not, ask for it to be put on a future agenda.
- Find out if your LEA is running any awareness sessions.
- Discover if it has been discussed by the staff.

Even if your head teacher or your colleagues are unwilling to take the index on board, it is important that you as a governing body set aside some time to explore the issues of inclusion. At the same time you will need to pay particular attention to the requirements of the SEN and Disability Act 2001 and the *Disability Code of Practice* shortly to be issued by the Disability Rights Commission to accompany it. This is a totally separate document from the revised *Code of Practice on the Identification and Assessment of Pupils with Special Educational Needs* (DfES 2001). However, it has far-reaching implications which you as special needs governor will have to bring to the attention of your colleagues.

Disability discrimination and the new act

The SEN and Disability Act 2001 is a landmark piece of legislation in that it extends the Disability Discrimination Act of 1995 to cover all aspects of education. The earlier act was drawn up on the assumption that the rights of children with disabilities were already safeguarded by the 1993 Education Act and the Code of Practice which followed it. In the last few years, however, it has become increasingly clear that this is not the case and that further legislation was required. Hence the new act which comes into force in September 2002.

Clark is a young man with significant learning difficulties. When he started at his primary school he was given full-time support. Over the next two years he made steady progress and it was agreed that his support should be cut from 25 to 20 hours per week in Year 2. Clark's teacher raised no objections and his parents were happy that he was doing so well. However, within a few days of the change, Clark's parents received a letter from the school informing them that the governors were not prepared to allow him to remain on the school premises without individual support. As a consequence, it would be necessary for his parents to collect him at 2pm each day, when his LSA finished work, and take him home.

Sadly, discrimination such as this is all too common and is frequently condoned by parents who are frightened to make a fuss for fear that their child will be rejected and their mainstream place withdrawn. The purpose of the Act is to provide protection for disabled pupils by making discrimination on the basis of their disability unlawful. Under this legislation, schools have two primary duties:

1. Not to treat disabled pupils less favourably than their able-bodied peers and
2. To make reasonable adjustments to avoid putting disabled pupils at a substantial disadvantage.

In this respect, governors are responsible not only for their own actions but also for those of people employed by them or working with the school's authority.

The Education Act 1996 already places a duty on governors to explain their admission arrangements for disabled pupils in their annual report to parents. However, the SEN and Disability Act 2001 goes a lot further in stating that governors may no longer discriminate against disabled children:

(a) in setting the criteria they use for deciding who will be admitted to the school when it is oversubscribed
(b) in the terms on which pupils are offered admission to the school or
(c) by refusing an application from someone because of their disability.

Daisy is a young lady with a diagnosis of autism. She successfully attended a local nursery school and her parents were keen for her to continue to be included at primary level. The LEA was supportive but made it clear that it was up to the parents to find a suitable school. Once the school agreed to admit Daisy, additional resources would be provided. So the parents began to approach local schools. Many were welcoming initially, but each in turn rejected her application on the grounds that they did not have the expertise or the resources to meet her needs. Although understandable, such behaviour on the part of the governors is clearly discriminatory under the Act. The only justifiable reason for rejecting Daisy would have been if the school was full. Even then she would have had the same right of appeal as any other pupil.

Under the Act, governors must make sure that disabled children are treated no less favourably than their peers in relation to:

- the curriculum
- teaching and learning
- classroom organisation
- timetabling
- pupil grouping
- homework
- access to school facilities
- school sports
- breaks and lunchtimes
- interaction with peers
- assessment and exam arrangements
- school discipline and sanctions
- school clubs and after-school activities
- school trips.

In looking at areas of school life where pupils may feel discriminated against, you need to address the following three questions.

1. Is the disabled pupil being treated less favourably than their able-bodied peers?

2. Is this less favourable treatment related to the student's disability?

3. Can this treatment be justified or could alternative adjustments be made?

Look at the following scenarios and decide whether you think the school is guilty of unjustified discrimination. Where this is the case, what alternative strategies could it use to overcome the problems?

- Mary has no arms. Despite being bright and enthusiastic she is placed in bottom sets as this is the only setting in which additional support is available.
- Tim's class is going on a trip. Tim, who is a wheelchair user, and his best friend have to stay behind because they failed to complete the work set the previous week.
- Mark's year group is off for an outward bound weekend. Mark has Down's Syndrome. Despite his parent's wishes for him to be fully included he is denied a place because his learning supporter is not available to accompany him.
- Daryl has cerebral palsy and needs to be exercised on a weekly basis. Her physiotherapist is only able to come into school on a Friday afternoon so Daryl has to miss singing which she really enjoys.
- Sammy is profoundly and multiply disabled. When her class goes swimming she has to sit and watch, although she loves the water, because the pool's swimming instructor refuses to accept responsibility for her.

In seeking to justify less favourable treatment, you will need to discover whether all reasonable adjustments have been explored. However, none of us can be perfect and there will almost certainly be situations where justifications can be found. As the *Draft Code of*

Practice (Disability Rights Commission 2001) notes, making reasonable adjustments does not require the governing body to provide auxiliary aids and services. Nor does it require them to make alterations to the physical features of the school.

Schools cannot make necessary adjustments unless they are provided with reliable and up-to-date information about the child's disability. They also must have regard to:

- the need to maintain academic, musical and sporting standards
- the cost of taking a particular step and the resources available to the school
- the extent to which it is practicable to take a particular step
- health and safety requirements and the interests of other pupils.

While it is clearly necessary to inform the whole school of the requirements of the Act as it relates to existing school pupils, it is also important to make it clear that the duties are anticipatory and relate to disabled children in general. Therefore, whether you currently cater for a number of disabled pupils or not, it would be wise for you as a governing body to look at your existing policies and procedures to ensure that no disabled pupil admitted to your school in the future is placed at a substantial disadvantage.

Developing effective school policies

All schools are encouraged to develop policies. However, as Shuttleworth (2000) notes it is what actually happens in a school that matters, not a filing cabinet full of pristine policy documents. Policies should never sit on shelves gathering dust, but should be constantly reviewed and updated. In this the whole school community should have a part to play, as policy will only influence practice if all those involved have ownership of the process. The role of the governors is to set the scene and determine the direction in which they see the school moving. It is also up to them to initiate and oversee the policy development process.

The number and range of policies will vary from school to school. While some are optional, others are mandatory and should be central to the work of the school. One of these is the policy that relates to SEN. The Education Act 1996 requires governing bodies, with the head teacher, to:

(a) develop a whole-school policy for SEN
(b) publish it in the school prospectus and
(c) inform parents about the success of the policy in the governor's annual report.

Governors' policy decisions about children with SEN are among the most important they are likely to make. If you are committed to helping your school become more inclusive, your involvement in the development of the SEN policy is crucial. Take a look at your existing policy and ask yourself the following questions:

- When was it first written and when was it last reviewed?
- Does it encapsulate your school's philosophy towards disabled pupils and the progress you are making towards becoming more inclusive?

If it is some time since it was last updated, this might be a good time to suggest a full policy review. 'Setting out to review and rewrite your SEN policy is an important opportunity as well as a positive and visible step forward in the life of the school' (Rogers 1996). The first step is to set up a working party to include members with a diversity of interests and views on disability and SEN. Make sure that all those concerned with the life of the school – governors, teachers, support staff, parents and pupils – are consulted and that the group has the time and the opportunity to liaise with other schools and with outside 'experts'.

Over time it should be possible for the group to:

(a) develop a shared vision
(b) carry out a special needs audit and so build a picture of where your school is now
(c) set realistic targets for school development.

Rogers (1996) suggests that in becoming more inclusive schools should focus on

- changing attitudes towards disabled pupils
- acquiring resources to guarantee the policy works
- making the school environment accessible to all
- spreading expertise among the staff
- developing activities for all children.

In producing the final policy, your working group needs to ensure that it meets the requirements laid down in the regulations (see Figure 9.1). At the same time, they need to write it in such a way that it highlights good inclusive practice. One of the problems in producing a policy to promote inclusion is that 'inclusive education' is not just another name for 'special educational needs'. As the authors of the *Index for Inclusion* (Booth *et al.* 2000) stress, it involves a different approach to identifying and attempting to resolve the difficulties that arise in schools.

The traditional approach to SEN can in fact be a barrier to the development of inclusive practices in schools by:

- conferring labels on students that can lead to lowered expectations
- focusing on the difficulties faced by categorised students and hence ignoring the problems faced by others
- encouraging some teachers to think that the education of students categorised as having SEN is primarily the responsibility of specialists.

Nevertheless, the concept of SEN remains part of the culture and policy framework of all schools. Although the inclusion debate makes us think about educational difficulties in rather different

1. Basic information about the school's special educational provision:
- the objectives of the SEN policy
- the name of the school's SEN coordinator or teacher responsible for day-to-day operation of the SEN policy
- the arrangements for coordinating educational provision for SEN pupils
- admission arrangements
- any SEN specialism and any special units
- any special facilities which increase or assist access to the school.

2. Information about the school's policies for identification, assessment and provision for all pupils with special needs:
- the allocation of resources to and among pupils with SEN
- identification and assessment arrangements and review procedures
- arrangements for providing access for pupils with SEN to a balanced and broadly based curriculum, including the National Curriculum
- how children with SEN are included within the school as a whole
- criteria for evaluating the success of the school's SEN policy
- arrangements for considering complaints about SEN provision.

3. Information about the school's staffing policies and partnership with bodies beyond the school:
- the school's arrangements for SEN in-service training
- use made of teachers and facilities from outside the school, including support services
- arrangements for partnership with parents
- links with other mainstream schools and special schools, including arrangements when pupils change schools or leave school
- links with health and social services, education welfare services and any voluntary organisations.

Figure 9.1 SEN policy requirements

ways, it is possible to hold onto the concept of breaking down barriers to learning and participation during the policy development process. An inclusive SEN policy will stress that SEN is a whole-school responsibility and that all teachers are teachers of pupils with special needs. In the inclusive school, learning support is a service for the whole school not just for pupils on the SEN Register or with statements. In explaining the arrangements for coordinating support it is useful to point out that all staff and governors have a role in ensuring that provision is used to promote inclusion.

Part of the process of policy review must address the interface between one school policy and another. In rewriting your SEN policy it is important to look at other existing policies, e.g for admissions, for behaviour, or for the curriculum, to ensure that there are no conflicts or contradictions. Think carefully about the benefits of combining your SEN and behaviour policies or about creating one overriding policy for inclusion or equal opportunities. Above all, take care to bear in mind any new legal requirements arising from the SEN and Disability Act 2001 and look carefully at the revised Code of Practice before you finalise your policy.

However assiduously your SEN working group carries out its duties and however thoughtfully it revises your policy, the test of any policy is the ease with which it can be implemented. Although it is the SENCO's responsibility to put the policy into practice, you as governors have the duty to report to parents on its success. It is therefore vital that monitoring and evaluation are seen as part of the implementation process. Key to this is the relationship built up between you as SEN governor and your SENCO. In their review of the role of the SENCO (DfEE 1998b), the research team found that in many schools the relationship was mutually supportive. 'However some SENCOs reported variable relationships with their governors and designated governors in turn reported variable states of preparation and access to necessary information for carrying out their role.'

It is relatively easy to monitor practical procedures. On the other hand, it is far harder to assess the impact of a policy on the philosophy or ethos of the school. However, governors who commit themselves to spending time in the school and meeting with the SENCO on a regular basis should be in a good position to do so. In looking at the impact of the SEN policy on pupils, discussion could usefully centre around the success of the various procedures and practices in promoting their participation in the curriculum and the life of the school. OFSTED (2000) in their guidance on evaluating educational inclusion suggest that inspectors ask three questions:

1. Do all pupils get a fair deal at school?
2. How well does the school recognise and overcome barriers to learning?
3. Do the school's values embrace inclusion and does its practice promote it?

As you evaluate the effectiveness of your school's policies, these might be good questions to hold onto. Above all you need to remember that, as OFSTED state:

> The most effective schools do not take educational inclusion for granted. They constantly monitor and evaluate the progress each pupil makes. They identify any pupils who may be missing out, difficult to engage, or feeling in some way to be apart from what the school seeks to provide. They take practical steps – in the classroom and beyond – to meet pupil needs effectively and they promote tolerance and understanding in a diverse society.

Resourcing for inclusion

Wertheimer (1997) in her booklet *Inclusive Education: a Framework for Change* comments that 'Resources – or lack of them – are continually used as a reason for inaction on inclusion. But underlying this is often a lack of commitment to change.' However, the UNESCO Salamanca Statement (1994) points out that 'within inclusive schools, children with special needs should receive whatever extra supports they require to ensure their effective education'.

The revised Code of Practice (DfES 2001) makes it clear that governors have a duty:

- to possess an up-to-date knowledge of the school's provision, including how funding, equipment and personnel resources are deployed
- to ensure that SEN provision is an integral part of the school development plan
- to continually monitor the quality of SEN provision.

In reviewing your provision, the *Index for Inclusion* (Booth *et al.* 2000) suggests that you ask two key questions:

1. What resources are currently available to support learning and participation?
2. How can additional resources be mobilised?

As part of your whole-school audit you will need to look at a whole range of issues (see Table 9.1).

In considering staffing arrangements, you will need to focus particularly on the model of support currently used in the school (see Lorenz 1998b). Do you tend to withdraw children from classes on a regular basis into a support base to be taught by specialist staff? If so this may be the time to look at developing more inclusive practices whereby students are supported in age-appropriate settings with typically developing peers or to consider employing learning supporters instead of specialist teachers. On the other hand, if support has been provided almost entirely by learning supporters with little status and no qualifications, it might be useful to focus on developing expertise in the support team and providing a career structure for staff.

Training is a key resourcing issue that must never be overlooked. Governors need to oversee the in-service education and training (INSET) programme and ensure that identified needs are met. Particular attention should be given to the distribution of funds and the allocation of supply cover to make sure that support assistants have the same access to training as teachers. Identify a variety of providers and encourage staff to train in groups or as a whole school as well as individually. It is important to involve all staff in training on inclusion and the use of support, not just those designated as having SEN responsibilities, as inclusion must be seen as a whole-school issue.

Staffing: How many teachers are currently employed and what is their expertise? How many learning supporters are currently employed and what qualifications do they possess? How are teaching and non-teaching staff currently deployed? Could personnel be deployed more effectively to increase student participation?
Training: What in-service training is currently being offered to teaching and support staff? Are there skill deficits which have been identified? What forms of additional training are required to rectify these deficits? Have appropriate training providers been located?
Access: Are all parts of the school building fully accessible? What building improvements should be included in the School Development Plan? Does the school have appropriate aids and adaptations to ensure curriculum access? What additional equipment is needed and how can it be obtained?
Curriculum: Is the curriculum suitably differentiated across the school to maximise access? Do teachers produce shared, recyclable resources to promote learning? Is there a centralised resource base or library? Do all staff know of the resources available to support learning in their lessons?
Outside links: Does the school have access to visiting specialists from LEA support services? Do students with health needs receive appropriate levels of professional support? Does the school work cooperatively with neighbouring mainstream or special schools? What additional links would be of benefit and how could they be developed?

Table 9.1 An audit of SEN provision

Most school buildings were erected at a point in time when nobody even considered the possibility of them catering for students in wheelchairs, with a profound hearing loss or significant visual impairment. It is, therefore, not surprising that many are totally unsuitable for full inclusion. On the other hand, the majority can, over time, be adapted and modified to significantly increase their suitability. Although the government expects all schools to work towards increasing the accessibility of their buildings, there is an understanding that this may take some time. Nevertheless, as governors you need to have a clear development plan.

In looking at curricular resources it is important to bear in mind the need for all teachers to interact with and plan for students with SEN. It is therefore not good enough for all resources to be retained by your SENCO or the support teaching team. In the primary school there should be a central resource where all staff can lodge copies of differentiated materials they have produced for use by others. In the secondary school, each department should have their own differentiated resources. In the same vein it is essential that learning supporters have access to appropriate resources rather than having to provide their own. An inclusive school should have a culture of sharing and support, not one of protectiveness and professional jealousy.

Finally, in auditing your resources, it is essential to look outside the school and enlist the help of as many outside agencies as you can. A recent report (Mencap 2001) revealed a lack of support and information for young people with health needs in mainstream settings. School nursing services have been significantly depleted and there is little guidance for schools on contentious areas such as the administration of medication. Similarly many schools find difficulty in accessing appropriate levels of physiotherapy or speech therapy. Try to build positive relationships, but think carefully about the role of outside 'experts'. Make sure that any links you set up are to the advantage of your pupils and promote inclusion rather then serving to deskill your staff or promote special and segregated approaches.

As Ainscow *et al.* (1999) note, the level of SEN funding within each LEA and the way it is distributed between schools has a direct bearing on progress towards inclusive practices. Funding schemes that rely largely on the distribution of funds via statements are probably the least helpful as they encourage schools to categorise an increasing number of children and cater for them on an individual basis. Conversely, schools in LEAs that fund generously using whole-school audits of need or indirect measures of deprivation, tend to statement fewer children and are able to focus on whole-school developments.

Research has shown that significant progress can be made without additional funding by redirecting existing resources. Nevertheless, as a governor it is important for you to be aware of any money coming into school which could be used to promote inclusion. In addition to funding for special needs coming directly from your LEA, there is now a series of additional grants for which you could apply. Details of the grants available can be found in the leaflet *Money for Inclusion* produced by the Centre for Studies in Inclusive Education (CSIE) (2001).

The Standards Fund is a collection of specific grants which enables schools to achieve improvements in educational standards set out in agreed targets, including those for inclusion. LEAs are required to make a contribution and then to devolve most of this money to schools. Because of the financial commitment not all LEAs will apply for Standards Fund monies, however most will. Grant 202 supports the creation of more inclusive schools via individual projects that will prepare schools and LEAs for their new responsibilities under the revised Code of Practice (DfES 2001) and the SEN and Disability Act 2001. The money can be used to develop new initiatives or to fund training for teachers and learning supporters.

In contrast, the Schools Access initiative is designed to improve access to mainstream schools for pupils with disabilities. Again the money is distributed via LEAs who must confirm their wish to take up their allocation. Projects under the Access Initiative can focus on improving physical access to the school through the provision of lifts and ramps, or on improving ease of movement around the building for pupils with mobility problems or sensory difficulties. Monies can be used to provide adapted toilets, sound proofing or treatment rooms. They can also be used to increase the access of disabled students to the curriculum through the provision of appropriate technology, aids and adaptations.

It has been said that inclusion is the keystone of government education policy (DfEE 1998a). However, you must never forget that it is a long road or underestimate the real challenges schools face in becoming more inclusive. On the other hand, you must hold onto the belief that 'regular schools with this inclusive orientation are the most effective means of combating discriminatory attitudes, creating welcoming communities, building an inclusive society and achieving education for all' (UNESCO 1994).

References

Ainscow, M. (1995) 'Special needs through school improvement: school improvement through special needs', in Clark, C., Dyson, A. and Millward, A. (eds) *Towards Inclusive Schools?* London: David Fulton Publishers.

Ainscow, M., Farrell, P., Tweddle, D. and Malki, G. (1999) *Effective Practice in Inclusion and in Special and Mainstream Schools Working Together.* London: DfEE.

Alderson, P. (ed.) (1999) *Learning and Inclusion: The Cleves School Experience.* London: David Fulton Publishers.

Alliance for Inclusive Education (AIE) (2001) *The Inclusion Assistant.* London: AIE.

Armstrong, F. (1998) 'Curricula, management and special and inclusive education', in Clough. P. (ed.) *Managing Inclusive Education.* London: Paul Chapman Publishing.

Ashley's mom (2001) *Designing Dynamic Student Portfolios.* www.ashleysmom.com/studentportfolios.htm

Aspis, S. (2000) *Disabled Children with Learning Difficulties Fight for Inclusion:* London: Changing Perspectives.

Babbage, R., Byers, R. and Redding, H. (eds.) (1999) *Approaches to Teaching and Learning: Including Pupils with Learning Difficulties.* London: David Fulton Publishers.

Balshaw, M. (1999) *Help in the Classroom.* London: David Fulton Publishers.

Barrow, G. (1998) *Disaffection and Inclusion: Merton's mainstream approach to difficult behaviour.* Bristol: Centre for Studies in Inclusive Education (CSIE).

Beadman, J. (1997) *An evaluation of educational placement for children with Down's syndrome in the South Devon area.* Torquay: Devon Education Department.

Beresford, P. and Tuckwell, P. (1978) *Schools for All.* London: Mind (National Association for Mental Health).

Berger, A. and Gross, J. (1999) *Teaching the Literacy Hour in an Inclusive Classroom.* London: David Fulton Publishers.

Booth, T., Ainscow, M., Black-Hawkins, K., Vaughan, M. and Shaw, L. (2000) *Index for Inclusion.* Bristol: Centre for Studies in Inclusive Education (CSIE).

Buckley, S., Bird, G., Sachs, B. and Archer, T. (2000) 'A comparison of mainstream and special school education for teenagers with Down's Syndrome', *Down's Syndrome Research and Practice* **7**(1).

Capper, S. (1999) *SENT Ahead.* Woodbridge: Independent Panel for Special Educational Advice (IPSEA).

Centre for Studies in Inclusive Education (CSIE) (2001) *Money for Inclusion.* Bristol: CSIE.

Croll, P. and Moses, D. (2000) *Special Needs in the Primary School.* London: Cassell.

Cullen. M., *et al.* (2001) *Letting Talents Shine: Guidance on Using Alternative Curriculum Programmes at Key Stage 4.* Slough: National Foundation for Educational Research (NFER).

Cumine, V., Leach, J. and Stevenson, G. (1998) *Asperger's Syndrome.* London: David Fulton Publishers.

Curry, M. and Broomfield, C. (1994) *Personal and Social Education for Primary Schools through Circle Time.* Tamworth: National Association for Special Educational Needs (NASEN).

Department for Education and Employment (DfEE) (1994) *Code of Practice on the Identification and Assessment of Special Educational Needs.* London: HMSO.

Department for Education and Employment (DfEE) (1997) *Excellence for All Children: Meeting Special Educational Needs.* London: HMSO.

Department for Education and Employment (DfEE) (1998a) *Meeting Special Educational Needs: A Programme of Action.* London: HMSO.

Department for Education and Employment (DfEE) (1998b) *The Role of the SENCO.* London: HMSO.

Department for Education and Employment (2000) *Roles of Governing Bodies and Head Teachers.* London: HMSO.

Department for Education and Employment (2001a) *Working with Teaching Assistants.* London: HMSO.

Department for Education and Employment (2001b) *Teaching Assistant File.* London: HMSO.

Department for Education and Skills (DfES) (2001) *The Revised Code of Practice on the Identification and Assessment of Pupils with Special Educational Needs.* London: HMSO.

Department of Health and Social Security (DHSS) (1991) *The Children Act 1989: Guidance and Regulation.* London: HMSO.

Dew-Hughes, D. (1999) 'Research summary – the social development of children in special schools', *Down's Syndrome News & Update* **1**(1).

Dew-Hughes, D. and Blandford, S. (1998) 'The social development of children with severe learning difficulties', *Down's Syndrome Research & Practice* **6**(1).

Disability Rights Commission (2001) *Draft Code of Practice (Schools).* Consultation document. London: DRC.

Disability Rights Task Force (1999) *From Exclusion to Inclusion.* London: DfEE.

Doyle, M. (1997) *The Paraprofessionals Guide to the Inclusive Classroom.* Baltimore: Paul Brookes Publishing.

Doyle, M. and Lee, P. (2000) 'Creating partnerships with paraprofessionals', in Giangreco, M. (ed.) *Quick Guides to Inclusion* (1). Baltimore: Paul Brookes Publishing.

Elton, Lord *Discipline in Schools*. London: HMSO.

England, J. (2001) Personal communication.

Evans, P. (1997) in Pijl, S., Meijer, C. and Hegarty, S. (eds) *Inclusive Education: A Global Agenda*. London: Routledge.

Foot, H., Morgan, M. and Shute, R. (1990) *Children Helping Children*. London: John Wiley.

Fox, G. (1998) *A Handbook for Learning Support Assistants*. London: David Fulton Publishers.

Fox, G. and Halliwell, M. (2000) *Supporting Literacy and Numeracy*. London: David Fulton Publishers.

Fullan, M. (1991) *The New Meaning of Educational Change*. London: Cassell.

Giangreco, M. (1997) 'Including students with disabilities in the classroom', in Giangreco, M. (ed.) *Quick Guides to Inclusion* 1. Baltimore: Paul Brookes Publishing.

Giangreco, M., Cloninger, C. and Iverson, V. (1998) *Choosing Outcomes and Accommodations for Children*. Baltimore: Paul Brookes Publishing.

Gross, J. (2000) 'Paper promises? Making the Code work for you', *Support for Learning* **15**(3), 126–34.

Hittie, M. (2000) 'Building community in the classroom', paper presented at the International Education Summit, Detroit, Michigan.

Hopkins, D. (1997) *Creating the Conditions for Classroom Improvement*. London: David Fulton Publishers.

Howson, J. (2000) 'Special needs demand swells', *Times Educational Supplement*, 15 December.

Hutchinson, A. (2001) *Curriculum Maps*. Hillingdon: Hedgewood School.

Jupp, K. (1992) *Everyone Belongs*. London: Souvenir Press.

Kenward, H. (1997) *Integrating Pupils with Disabilities in Mainstream Schools: Making it Happen*. London: David Fulton Publishers.

Kunc, N. (1984) 'Integration: being realistic isn't realistic', *Canadian Journal for Exceptional Children* **1**(1).

Lang, G. and Berberich, C. (1995) *All Children Are Special*. Armadale: Eleanor Curtain Publishing.

Lee, B. and Henkhuzens, Z. (1996) *Integration in Progress*. Slough: National Foundation for Educational Research (NFER).

Long, R. (1999) *Friendships*. Tamworth: National Association for Special Educational Needs (NASEN).

Lorenz, S. (1998a) *Children with Down's Syndrome*. London: David Fulton Publishers.

Lorenz, S. (1998b) *Effective In-Class Support*. London: David Fulton Publishers.

Lorenz, S. (1999a) *Experiences of Inclusion for Children with Down's Syndrome*. London: Down's Syndrome Association.

Lorenz, S. (1999b) *Supporting Support Assistants.* Manchester: Downright Press.
Lorenz, S. (2001) *The Support Assistant's Survival Guide.* Manchester: Downright Press.
Manolson, A. (1992) *It Takes Two to Talk.* Bicester: Winslow Press.
Marvin, C. (1998) 'Individual and whole class teaching', in Tilstone, C., Florian, L. and Rose, R. (eds) *Promoting Inclusive Practice.* London: Routledge.
Mason, M. (2000) *Incurably Human.* London: Working Press.
McPherson, W. (1999) *The Stephen Lawrence Enquiry.* London: HMSO.
Mencap (2001) *Don't Count Me Out.* London: Mencap.
Morris, J. (1998) *Still Missing – Who Cares?* London: Trust.
Moseley, J. and Tew, M. (1999) *Quality Circle Time in the Secondary School.* London: David Fulton Publishers.
Munn, P., Lloyd, G. and Cullen, M. (2000) *Alternatives to Exclusion from School.* London: Paul Chapman.
Murray, P. and Penman, J. (eds) (1996) *Let Our Children Be.* Sheffield: Parents with Attitude.
MVDP (2000) *Makaton Make and Do.* Bicester: Winslow Press.
National Association for Special Educational Needs (NASEN) (2000) *Consultation Paper: Proposed Revision of SEN Code of Practice.* Tamworth: NASEN.
O'Brien, J. and Forest, M. (1998) *Action for Inclusion.* Toronto: Inclusion Press.
Office for Standards in Education (OFSTED) (2000) *Evaluating Educational Inclusion.* London: HMSO.
Parsons, C. (1999) *Education, Exclusion and Citizenship.* London: Routledge.
Peterson, M. and Tamor, L. (2001) *Authentic Multilevel Teaching in Understanding Best Practices for All.* Whole Schooling Research Project, Detroit, Michigan.
Postman, N. (1996) *The End of Education.* New York: Alfred A. Knopf.
Qualifications and Curriculum Authority (QCA) (2000) *Early Learning Goals.* London: HMSO.
Reif, S. and Heimburge, J. (1996) *How to Reach and Teach All Students in the Inclusive Classroom.* New York: Prentice Hall International.
Roffey, S. (1999) *Special Needs in the Early Years.* London: David Fulton Publishers.
Rogers, R. (1996) *Developing an Inclusive Policy for Your School.* Bristol: Centre for Studies in Inclusive Education (CSIE).
Rose, R. (1998) The curriculum: a vehicle for inclusion or a level for exclusion?, in Tilstone, C., Florian, L. and Rose, R. (eds) *Promoting Inclusive Practice.* London: Routledge.
Royal National Institute for the Blind (2000) *Shaping the Future.* London: RNIB.
Sebba, J. and Sachdev, D. (1997) *What Works in Inclusive Education?* London: Barnardo's.
Shaw, L. (2001) *Learning Supporters and Inclusion.* Bristol: Centre for Studies in Inclusive Education (CSIE).

Shuttleworth, V. (2000) *The Special Educational Needs Coordinator.* London: Pearson Education.

Skrtic, T. (1991) 'The special education paradox', *Harvard Educational Review* **61**(2).

Smith, I. (1998) *Is Praise Always a Good Thing?* Edinburgh: Scottish Consultative Council on the Curriculum.

Sukhnandan, L. and Lee, B. (1998) *Streaming, Setting and Grouping by Ability: A review of literature.* Slough: National Foundation for Educational Research (NFER).

Tashie, C., Shapiro-Barnard, S., Dillon, A., Schuh, M., Jorgensen, C. and Nisbet, J. (1993) *Changes in Latitudes, Changes in Attitudes.* Concord: University of New Hampshire.

Teacher Training Agency (TTA) (1998) *National Standards for Special Educational Needs Coordinators.* London: HMSO.

Thomas, G. (1999) Foreword, in Babbage, R., Byers, R. and Redding, H. *Approaches to Teaching and Learning: Including Pupils with Learning Difficulties.* London: David Fulton Publishers.

Thomas, G. and Loxley, A. (2001) *Deconstructing Special Education and Constructing Inclusion.* Buckingham: Open University Press.

Thomas, G., Walker, D. and Webb, J. (1998) *The Making of the Inclusive School.* London: Routledge.

United Nations Educational, Scientific and Cultural Organization (UNESCO) (1994) *The Salamanca Statement.* Paris: UNESCO.

Wertheimer, A. (1997) *Inclusive Education: a Framework for Change.* Bristol: Centre for Studies in Inclusive Education (CSIE).

Wilson, C. and Jade, R. (1999) *Whose Voice Is it Anyway?* London: Alliance for Inclusive Education (AIE).

Wilson, D. and Newton, C. (1999) *Circle of Friends.* Dunstable: Folens.

Wilson, H. (1998) *Moving Towards Inclusion.* Birmingham: Birmingham City Council.

Wolger, J. (1998) 'Managing change', in Tilstone, C., Florian, L. and Rose, R. (eds) *Promoting Exclusive Practice.* London: Routledge

Wright, J. and Ruebain, D. (2000) *Taking Action.* Birmingham: Questions Publishing.

Zemelman, S. (1998) Best Practice: *New Standards for Teaching and Learning in America's Schools.* London: Heinemann.

Index